J 994.04 COUP
Coupe, Robert.
Achieving nationhood : the sto
ACC 0181501
BRN 123788

G000139811

ACHIEVING NATIONHOOD

The Story of Federation

RETURN ON OR BEFORE
LAST DATE MARKED

- 3 NOV 2000
- 3 JUL 2001

CANCELLED

ACHIEVING
NATIONHOOD

The Story of Federation

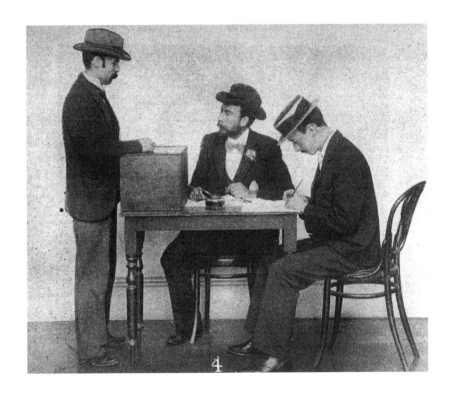

*Macquarie
Regional Library*

ROBERT COUPE

NEW
HOLLAND

First published in Australia in 2000 by
New Holland Publishers (Australia) Pty Ltd
Sydney • Auckland • London • Cape Town
14 Aquatic Drive Frenchs Forest NSW 2086 Australia
218 Lake Road Northcote Auckland New Zealand
24 Nutford Place London W1H 6DQ United Kingdom
80 McKenzie Street Cape Town 8001 South Africa

Copyright © 2000 in text: Robert Coupe
Copyright © 2000 in maps: New Holland Publishers (Australia) Pty Ltd
Copyright © 2000 in photographs as credited below
Copyright © 2000 New Holland Publishers (Australia) Pty Ltd

All rights reserved. No part of this publication may be reproduced,
stored in a retrieval system or transmitted, in any form or by any means,
electronic, mechanical, photocopying, recording or otherwise,
without the prior written permission of the publishers and copyright holders.

National Library of Australia Cataloguing-in-Publication Data:

Coupe, Robert.
    Achieving Nationhood: the story of Federation

    Includes index.
    ISBN 1 86436 546 3.

    Federal government—Australia—History—20th century—Juvenile literature.
    Australia—Politics and government—20th century—Juvenile literature.
    Australia—History—Juvenile literature.
    I. Title

    994.04

Publishing General Manager: Jane Hazell
Publisher: Averill Chase
Editor: Marie-Claire Muir
Design Concept: Patricia McCallum
Cover Design and Layout: Jenny Mansfield
Picture Researcher: Kirsti Wright
Reproduction: Dot'n'Line
Printer: Kyodo, Singapore

Cover Photos

Front Cover: Henry Parkes and delegates to the 1890 federation conference.
Back Cover: The Centennial International Exhibition building of Melbourne.

Picture Acknowledgements
All images National Library of Australia with the exception of:
—Mitchell Library, State Library of NSW: pp3, 13, 59
—State Library of Victoria: pp22, 46
—Anthony Johnson/New Holland Image Library: p62
—AAP: p63
—Image on p26 reproduced with the permission
  of the Library Committee of the Parliament of Victoria.

CONTENTS

A Day of Celebration

The first day of January 1901 was not just the beginning of a new century; it was a day of special celebration for most people in the Australian colonies. This was the day on which the six Australian colonies of Great Britain officially combined to form the new independent nation of Australia. The six former colonies were combining because at referendums held over the previous two years, a majority of voters in each colony had voted in favour of federation. Each of the six colonies would be a state in the new Commonwealth of Australia. Although Australia would now have its own government and would no longer be subject to the British government, the English monarch, who was then Queen Victoria, would remain Australia's head of state. She and her successors were to be represented in Australia by a person known as the governor-general.

Ceremonies and festivals were organised in cities and towns right around the country, but the main celebrations were in Sydney, the capital of New South Wales. They centred on Centennial Park, on the eastern outskirts of the city. Here, in a highly ornate plaster pavilion, at one o'clock in the afternoon, the governor-general, a Scotsman called Lord Hopetoun, read a proclamation and signed documents that declared Australia to be an independent nation. Then, he swore in the country's first prime minister, Edmund Barton, and members of his government.

A grand occasion

A crowd of more than 70 000 people watched the ceremony in Centennial Park that sunny summer afternoon. Many thousands more lined the colourfully decorated streets between the Domain, a large green space near the centre of the city, and Centennial Park. They were there to watch a grand procession that included shearers on horseback, soldiers, firemen, politicians and the governor-general. Many of the people had been up all night after noisily seeing in the first new year of the new century. Some of them had bought tickets, and sat comfortably in specially constructed stands. Most crowded along the footpaths, straining for a glimpse of the passing parade, the brass bands and other entertainments that were provided for the occasion. They waved flags and shouted excitedly as the parade passed by.

At the end of the ceremony in Centennial Park, a huge choir of 10 000 schoolgirls sang a rousing anthem and soldiers fired guns in the air to salute the arrival of the new commonwealth. The festivities continued throughout the afternoon and evening as hundreds of schoolchildren performed traditional English dances at the Sydney Cricket Ground, and there were brilliant fireworks displays.

That evening there was a lavish banquet attended by politicians, church and military

Lord Hopetoun swearing in Edmund Barton as Australia's first prime minister.

dignitaries and other powerful and influential people. Missing from the banquet was Lord Hopetoun. He was too ill to attend. On his way to Australia from England, he had stayed for a short time in India, where he had caught typhoid fever.

Many other people also had a better meal than usual that night. More than 7000 poor families were given coupons which they could exchange for food.

For and against federation

While most Australians were happy that Australia had finally become one nation, there were still many people who were not in favour of federation. For more than 10 years there had been fierce debates about federation, and we will look at the arguments for and against federation later in this book.

When Lord Hopetoun arrived in Sydney in the middle of December 1900, one of his jobs was to invite somebody to head the government and become Australia's first prime minister. Possibly because he was still very sick, he made a very unwise choice. He invited Sir William Lyne, the premier of New South Wales, to form a government. He probably did not know at this stage that Lyne was one of the strongest opponents of federation. Other politicians,

Sir Edmund Barton.

however, who of course knew Lyne's opinions, refused to serve in a government with him. That was why Hopetoun turned to Edmund Barton, another New South Wales politician, who was a passionate supporter of federation. When the first Australian elections were held at the end of March 1901, Barton's government was confirmed in office and he remained prime minister until 1903.

Melbourne's turn

Melbourne's turn for lavish celebrations came just a few months later, in May 1901, when the first Australian parliament was opened there. At that stage, the place where Canberra now stands was open grazing country, and no-one could have guessed that it would later be chosen as the site of Australia's national capital. It was not until 1927 that the Australian parliament moved from Melbourne to the tiny new city on the Molonglo River, almost exactly half way between the rival cities of Sydney and Melbourne.

A Sydney street decorated for the federation celebrations.

GOVERNORS AND SOLDIERS

By 1890, all of the six British colonies that later joined together to form the new Commonwealth of Australia had governments and parliaments of their own. Although they were still officially subject to the British government, in most matters these colonies were independent and free to make their own laws.

In the early days of modern Australian history—after 1788, when the first convict settlement was established on the banks of Sydney Harbour and the colony of New South Wales was declared—a series of 'governors' ran the colony. These were men appointed by the British government to make laws, to command the soldiers who guarded and supervised the convicts and to maintain law and order. The governor, especially at first, was the most powerful person in the colony, with authority over everyone in the settlement. Governors could have convicts flogged, imprisoned, and even hanged, for a wide range of crimes. Within weeks of the First Fleet's arrival in New South Wales, the first governor, Captain Arthur Phillip, who was generally thought to be not a harsh man, ordered a convict to be hanged for stealing food, and during the rest of the year another four convicts died in the same way. In March 1789 Phillip made an example of six soldiers who were caught stealing food by having them publicly hanged.

Sharing power

As the colony grew and expanded, and as more convicts and free settlers arrived from the other side of the world, more people became increasingly powerful in the colony. Magistrates were appointed to administer justice, and ambitious army officers, members of what was known as the New South Wales Corps, were able to influence important decisions. As the number of free settlers grew, groups of wealthy merchants and others were able to put pressure on governors to run the colony as they thought it should be run.

When Governor Phillip, ill and exhausted, sailed back to England at the end of 1892, there was no-one to replace him. For almost three years, until the next

Captain Arthur Phillip.

governor, John Hunter, arrived in September 1795, New South Wales was governed by army officers—members of the New South Wales Corps—first, Major Francis Grose, and then Captain William Paterson. Grose increased the power and influence of army officers in the colony by granting them land, encouraging them to establish farms on this land and assigning convicts to them to act as labourers on these farms. They also allowed these officers to pay the convicts who worked for them in rum.

Governors, officers, rum and John Macarthur

It was not long before rum became the main means of payment in the colony. In any case, there was very little real money in the form of coins. Most convicts were happy enough to be paid in rum, which was the only form of alcohol available in large quantities. It was, after all, about the only luxury they could get, and it helped many of them to forget for a while the miserable conditions in which they lived. Just as today, when those who control the supply of money are among the most powerful people in society, so the officers of the New South Wales Corps, who had control over the supply of rum, had considerable power and influence. It was not long before the New South Wales Corps became known more generally as the 'Rum Corps'. Often they defied the

Captain John Macarthur.

Governor William Bligh.

authority of the governors, who tried, without much success, to restrict their ability to trade in rum and to limit their power in other ways.

Governor John Hunter, who arrived in 1895, introduced a system of licences for those who distilled and traded in rum, but the Rum Corps ignored these regulations. Neither Hunter nor Philip Gidley King, who arrived to replace Hunter in 1800, were popular with the officers. As well as trying to crack down on the sale and distilling of rum, King clashed with one of the most influential men in the colony—an officer of the New South Wales Corps named John Macarthur.

In 1802, Macarthur injured his commanding officer in a duel, and King banished him from the colony and shipped him back to England. So powerful was Macarthur that King wrote to the British government, suggesting sarcastically that if Macarthur ever came back to New South Wales, it should be as governor. According to King, 'one half of the colony already belongs to him, and it will not be long before he gets the other half'. In 1805, Macarthur was back in New South Wales—not as governor, but no longer in disgrace. He brought with him orders from the British Government that Governor King was to grant him a large area of land on which to breed merino sheep. King had no choice but to obey the order.

Macarthur clashed even more seriously with the next governor, William Bligh, who arrived in

1806, and who immediately set about trying to stamp out the illegal trading in rum. This earned him the hatred of the Rum Corps and of Macarthur who, although he was no longer in the army, was still looked up to by many of the officers. Relations were not helped by the fact that the two men seemed to be natural enemies. Both were stubborn: Macarthur was domineering and always determined to get his own way; Bligh was impetuous and bad-tempered. The two men were always at loggerheads, and things came to a head when, in December 1807, Bligh had Macarthur arrested for a breach of regulations by the crew of a ship of which Macarthur was part owner.

Macarthur's trial took place on 25 January 1808, but it was chaotic, with Macarthur insulting the judges and calling one of them a swindler. It ended with no verdict and with Macarthur walking out. The next day, which was the anniversary of the first landing at Sydney Cove 20 years earlier, was a day of celebration for the Rum Corps. After hours of heavy drinking, a number of officers, led by Major George Johnston who was a close friend and ally of Macarthur and who was probably urged on by him, decided to take revenge on the governor. In the evening after dark, they went to Government House, forced their way in and placed the governor under arrest. Johnston declared himself lieutenant governor and took control of the colony. This incident is now generally known as the 'Rum Rebellion'.

Army officers, it seemed, were now the real rulers of New South Wales, and John Macarthur would always get his way.

A cartoon of 1808 showing the arrest of Governor William Bligh.

LACHLAN MACQUARIE—
A POWERFUL GOVERNOR

The next governor of New South Wales was Lachlan Macquarie. One of Sydney's grandest streets is named after him. He arrived in Sydney just over a year after the Rum Rebellion and officially became governor on New Year's Day, 1810. Bligh was now in Hobart Town in Van Diemen's Land, later renamed Tasmania. A separate convict settlement had been established here in 1804.

Immediately after his arrest, Bligh had been a prisoner in Government House for about two weeks. When, finally, his temper cooled and he agreed to sail to England, he was put aboard a ship, the *Porpoise*. Bligh immediately took command of this ship and sailed it, not back to England, but south to Hobart Town. His plan was to get the support of the lieutenant governor of the young settlement, Colonel David Collins. But Collins showed no interest in helping Bligh, so the deposed governor remained there for almost a year, until word reached him of the arrival in Sydney of Governor Macquarie. In January 1810, Bligh returned to Sydney where he sought Macquarie's help to gather evidence against those who had overthrown him, especially Johnston and Macarthur. Finally in May 1810, Bligh set sail at long last for England, bent on revenge.

Governor Lachlan Macquarie.

The revenge he got was not what he was looking for. Macarthur and Johnston sailed for England just a few months after the Rum Rebellion. Both no doubt feared they would be arrested and put on trial when a new governor arrived, and both were keen to explain to the British authorities that, by overthrowing Bligh, they were simply removing a man who had shown himself unfit to govern. Johnston, however, was charged with mutiny. Macarthur, possibly because he had many influential friends and supporters, was not charged. However, he was punished by being forced to remain in England, and be separated from his wife and five of his children. When, in 1811, Johnston stood trial on a charge of mutiny before a military court, he was found guilty. But instead of being sentenced to death, the usual penalty in those days for such a crime, he was merely dismissed from the army.

Eventually both Johnston and Macarthur returned to New South Wales—Johnston in 1813 and Macarthur, once he had been granted permission, late in 1817. Macarthur was allowed to return only on the condition that he took no part in public affairs—a condition he was destined not to fulfil. Just a few months after Macarthur arrived back, his old adversary Bligh died in London.

A powerful governor

Although after the Rum Rebellion the New South Wales Corps, or at least its commander, controlled the colony for about another year, its days were numbered. The new governor, Lachlan Macquarie, brought with him a new regiment, the 73rd Regiment, to enforce law and order in the colony, and the New South Wales Corps was disbanded. In May 1810, half its members sailed back to England: the others chose to stay in the colony, either as members of the new regiment, or as members of a special Veteran Corps which Macquarie set up for the longer-serving members.

Macquarie remained governor until 1820. Despite the many problems he encountered, Macquarie's term as governor is often thought of as a kind of golden age for the colony. A number of handsome buildings still standing in Sydney, and in some other parts of New South Wales, date from Macquarie's time and were commissioned by him. And Macquarie was probably the first governor to see Sydney, and the whole colony, as very much more than a penal settlement. He had a vision of Sydney as a fine city in which people could choose to live a productive and satisfying life. He encouraged convicts to develop and use their skills and to remain in the colony as free citizens when their sentences had expired. This brought Macquarie into conflict with many people who had come to New South Wales as free settlers, some of whom had become wealthy landowners or business people. These 'exclusives', as they called themselves, resented the fact that ex-convicts had the same rights and privileges as they did. But most of the time Macquarie got his way. Being the governor he did not have to answer to any other authority except the British government—and he did not have the officers of the New South Wales Corps to contend with.

Macquarie stays in charge

Two years after Lachlan Macquarie arrived in the colony, the British government appointed a committee to investigate conditions in the colony of New South Wales. The members of this committee reported favourably on Macquarie and the way he was governing the colony. They agreed with his policy of encouraging ex-convicts to stay on as free people in the colony—these people became known as 'emancipists'. However they did think that the governor had more power over the lives of people in the colony than any one person should have. They therefore suggested that a 'council' should be appointed to advise the governor and help him make important decisions.

Macquarie Street, Sydney, in the late 19th century.

Macquarie himself did not like this idea at all—in fact he hated it and argued strongly against it. He often consulted people he trusted about important decisions, but insisted that he must have the final say. He was not a man who liked to share authority. Luckily for him, Lord Bathurst, who held the title 'Secretary of State for the Colonies' in the British government, and who was therefore in charge of matters in New South Wales, did not think that such a council would work. It would be another 10 years—not until 1822 when Macquarie finally left the colony and returned to England—before the idea of a council to help and advise the governor would be considered again.

In another attempt to limit Macquarie's power, the committee suggested that he should not be allowed to pardon people convicted of criminal offences without getting permission from the British government. Macquarie did not like this either, even though Bathurst agreed with the committee about this. Macquarie argued with Bathurst that this would not work. After all, it would take months to get such permission, as letters would have to go back and forth across the seas. Bathurst finally agreed. As a result of the committee's report, then, Macquarie's power was not reduced and he continued to govern with almost complete authority in New South Wales. But he made many enemies who worked against him, especially free settlers and some officers who disliked Macquarie's policy of encouraging emancipists.

The convict barracks in Macquarie Street, Sydney, built during Macquarie's time as governor.

A LEGISLATIVE COUNCIL

Between 1872 and 1891, Sir Henry Parkes was five times, and for a total of 15 years, premier of the colony of New South Wales. He is often called the 'father of federation' because of his strong belief that the Australian colonies should unite to become an independent nation, and the important role he played in helping to make this happen. You will read more about him later in this book.

During the 1850s, soon after the beginning of Parkes' political career, he became a bitter opponent of another prominent citizen, William Charles Wentworth. Wentworth, who was by this time a rich landowner, a politician and a person of great influence in the colony, was strongly urging the British government to once again start sending convicts to New South Wales, a practice that had ceased in 1840. Convicts, argued Wentworth, would provide cheap labour and help in developing the colony. Parkes, and most other people in New South Wales, strongly opposed this idea and were successful in preventing it from being carried out. Wentworth angrily claimed that Parkes was an 'arch-anarchist'. Years later, however, long after Wentworth had died, Parkes paid him a great compliment, claiming that his efforts had helped to lay the groundwork for the federation of the Australian colonies.

When Wentworth died in 1872 at the age of 82, federation was no more than an idea in some people's heads. At this stage the idea had probably not even entered the heads of

Henry Parkes in 1850.

most people in the colonies. But by 1872 the colonies of New South Wales, Victoria, Tasmania, South Australia and Queensland—all except Western Australia—had their own parliaments, with at least some of their members elected, and their own constitutions—that is, documents that set out the rules for the governing of the colonies. These colonies had achieved what we call 'responsible government'. They made their own laws and were almost completely independent of the British government. Over many years William Charles Wentworth had played a vital role in helping to bring this about. If Parkes can be called the 'father of federation', Wentworth, more than any other person, deserves the title 'father of responsible government'.

An unpromising beginning

William Charles Wentworth was born in 1790 on board a convict ship sailing between Sydney and the convict settlement of Norfolk Island, where his mother, Catherine Crowley, was being transported for stealing clothing. His father, too, was on the ship. He was D'Arcy Wentworth, who had arrived in New South Wales with the Second Fleet and was going to Norfolk Island to work as a surgeon there. D'Arcy Wentworth was lucky not to have been going to Norfolk Island as a convict, or even not to have been hanged in England. He faced trial four times charged with highway robbery, but was never proven guilty.

William Charles Wentworth.

D'Arcy Wentworth prospered in New South Wales, becoming, among other things, chief surgeon, a magistrate and superintendent of police. He won the confidence of governors, including Macquarie, and was one of the founding directors of the Bank of New South Wales when it was established in 1816.

Making his way

Young William Charles Wentworth also showed early promise and achieved a number of notable firsts. In 1811, at the age of 21, Macquarie appointed him acting provost marshal, which meant that he was in charge of law and order in the colony. He was the first locally born person ever to be appointed to such an important post. Two years later, he achieved the first for which he is probably best known. Along with Gregory Blaxland and William Lawson, he led the first expedition that we know of to find a route across the Blue Mountains, west of Sydney. This was an important achievement as,

until that time, the colony had been unable to expand westwards beyond the barrier the mountains presented.

Three years after that, in 1816, Wentworth went to England to study law and advance his prospects. While he was there, he published, in 1819, the first book ever to be written by a native Australian. It was called *A statistical, historical and political description of New South Wales.* In this book, Wentworth explored many ideas about New South Wales and what he thought should happen there. Among the things he suggested was the appointment of a council, like the one that the British committee had suggested seven years earlier, to help the governor. But he went much further than this and suggested that a parliament, to be elected by men who owned property in the colony, even if they were former convicts, should rule the colony. He also suggested that trial by jury be introduced in New South Wales.

Bigge's report

In 1823, partly perhaps because of Wentworth's campaign, a Legislative Council was established. Other factors, of course, also played a part in bringing this council into existence. One of these was the growing dissatisfaction many settlers, such as John Macarthur, felt with the way Governor Macquarie was running the colony. Macarthur and other 'exclusivists' were especially angry about the favourable treatment Macquarie gave to former convicts, or 'emancipists', appointing them to positions of power and influence. They made their views known to the British government, which decided to hold an investigation into Macquarie's policies and the conditions in New South Wales.

In October 1819 John Thomas Bigge arrived in Sydney from England to begin his investigation. After almost 18 months in New South Wales, Bigge presented a report to the British government. In it he was very critical of many things, including Macquarie's lenient treatment of convicts and his policy towards the emancipists. Bigge's report almost broke Macquarie's heart. He considered it unfair, and referred to it as a 'vile and insidious document'. As well as this, he was by now an ill man, and asked to be allowed to return to England. In February 1822, just a year after Bigge had left the colony, Macquarie set sail for England. He died in Scotland just over two years later.

A Legislative Council is formed

Bigge's report did not actually recommend that a council be set up to help the governor govern, but it did draw attention to what Bigge and many of the powerful people in New South Wales saw as the dangers of having too

Governor Sir Thomas Brisbane.

much power in the hands of one man. Once again, Earl Bathurst considered the idea of a council. In July 1823, the British government passed an Act of Parliament setting up, among other things, a Legislative Council in New South Wales. This was the first step in limiting the governor's power, although at this stage it did not change it very much.

The council was to have between five and seven members, each of them appointed by the governor with the approval of the British government. Only the governor was allowed to propose new laws, and the governor needed only one other member of the council to bring a new law into being. Even in extreme cases, where the whole council opposed a new law, the governor could have his way. In effect, what the new arrangements ensured was that the governor at least had to seek the advice of the members of his council, even if he did not have to take that advice.

In 1828, the council was changed again. The number of members was increased to between 10 and 15, all still appointed by the governor. This time the governor's power was lessened. He could no longer go against the wishes of the council, or even a majority of its members. If the numbers for and against a new law proposed by the governor were even, he then had the casting vote.

John Macarthur, who, you will remember, was allowed to return to New South Wales in 1817 on the condition that he did not get involved in public affairs, was appointed a member of the Legislative Council when it was first set up in 1825 by Sir Thomas Brisbane, Macquarie's successor as governor. Brisbane left the colony in December 1825 and was succeeded by Sir Ralph Darling. Macarthur could

Governor Sir Ralph Darling.

not get on with the new governor, and he refused to attend meetings of the council. Despite this, he became a member of the new, expanded council in 1828. He quarrelled, too, with the next governor, Sir Richard Bourke, who arrived at the end of 1831. In fact, Macarthur, always a quarrelsome man, found it increasingly difficult to tolerate any views that were not the same as his own. During his long time in New South Wales, Macarthur clashed seriously with every governor except Brisbane. In 1832, Bourke had Macarthur removed from the legislative council, declaring him to be 'a lunatic'. Macarthur died two years later, almost friendless, his mind seriously unbalanced.

AN ELECTED COUNCIL

The young William Charles Wentworth was very ambitious. During his long public career, he fulfilled almost all his ambitions, but there was one that eluded him and that brought him into conflict with John Macarthur. Wentworth wanted to marry Macarthur's daughter, Elizabeth, but Macarthur opposed the marriage and forbade his daughter to have anything to do with Wentworth. Although he was now rich, Wentworth, according to Macarthur and other exclusives, was a descendant of convicts. His mother had been a convict and his father, who had been tried in England for highway robbery, was, according to many people in the colony, as good, or as bad, as one. It was even rumoured at one stage that Wentworth's father, D'Arcy Wentworth, had in fact come to the colony as a convict. To make matters even worse in Macarthur's eyes, Wentworth was a supporter of Governor Macquarie's policy of encouraging emancipists, or ex-convicts. Macarthur probably knew, too, that Wentworth had written some insulting verses about him and his fellow exclusives.

When Wentworth came back from England in 1824, he brought a printing press with him. He and Robert Wardell established a new newspaper in opposition to the *Sydney Gazette*, which was the official newspaper of the colony. The new newspaper was called the *Australian*. Right from the start the *Australian* supported the emancipists against the exclusives, which earned the paper, and Wentworth, the enmity of people like Macarthur. Instead of suppressing the new newspaper, as he could have done, Governor Brisbane, to the horror of the exclusives, decided to allow both the *Australian* and the *Sydney Gazette* full freedom.

Wentworth took full advantage of this freedom of speech. The *Australian* not only supported the rights of emancipists, it also agitated strongly for trial by jury in criminal cases and for an elected government for the colony. Wentworth also conducted public meetings. At one of these, in 1825, he described the exclusives who opposed him as 'yellow snakes of the colony' who were too frightened to allow the ordinary people of New South Wales the same rights that people in England enjoyed, including the right to elect those who made the laws. Wentworth's speech was duly reported in the *Australian*. Such strong language was typical of Wentworth, who was often hot-headed and frequently offended people whose views he opposed.

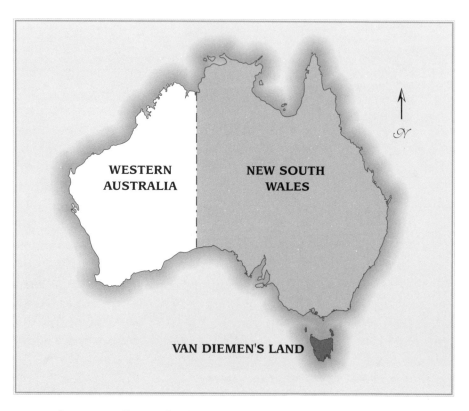

The Australian colonies in 1829, after Western Australia was declared a colony.

Democracy?

To us today, democracy means that every adult person has the right to vote in elections, and that every vote is worth as much as every other vote. We call this right of every adult to vote 'universal suffrage'. This is certainly not what William Charles Wentworth had in mind when he talked about an elected parliament. While he strongly defended the right of emancipists to have a vote, he believed that only men who owned land worth at least 200 pounds or who paid at least 10 pounds a year to rent a house—proving that they were people of 'substance'—should be allowed to vote. There was no thought at that time that women should be allowed to vote.

The Australian Patriotic Association

Movement towards an elected parliament did not seem to be getting anywhere, despite a number of public meetings and petitions organised by Wentworth and his supporters. In 1835, an organisation called the Australian Patriotic Association was formed to push the case for an elected parliament and for the right of emancipists to vote for its members. William Charles Wentworth was commissioned by this association to draft a 'constitution' for a self-governing colony. A constitution is a collection of rules or guidelines which spell out how an organisation, a country, or in this case the colony of New South Wales, must be run.

By the late 1830s public opinion in the colony was changing. Even wealthy people who had come to the colony as free immigrants began to believe that the people of the colony—or at least those who were reasonably wealthy—should have a say in choosing their government. By this time, too, there was less ill-feeling between the

In 1836 the colony of South Australia was founded. Its borders would later be extended.

free immigrants and the emancipists. Many emancipists had made good in the colony and had proved that they were capable of being good citizens. In a very curious alliance, William Charles Wentworth joined forces with James Macarthur, one of the sons of John Macarthur, to agitate in favour of an elected parliament.

Eventually, in 1842, the British parliament passed an Act, called the *Act for the Government of New South Wales and Van Diemen's Land*. Van Diemen's Land, which later became Tasmania, had been a separate colony since 1825. Two other colonies—South Australia and Western Australia—had also been founded by this time. Victoria and Queensland were still part of New South Wales, as was the present Northern Territory. New South Wales, then, occupied the whole of eastern Australia and most of central Australia, although most of this area was not yet populated by white settlers.

According to the 1842 Act of Parliament, the numbers in the New South Wales Legislative Council were to increase to 36 members. Twelve of these were to be appointed by the governor, with the approval of the British government, and the other 24 were to be elected. The people who could vote in elections were men who owned land worth at least 200 pounds, or who paid at least 20 pounds a year in rent. The Legislative Council was to last for five years, after which new elections were to be held and new councillors appointed. There were, however, to be no elected members to the Van Diemen's Land Legislative Council or to the Legislative Council of South Australia at this stage.

Still in charge

The new New South Wales Legislative Council held its first meeting in August 1843. Among the elected members were William Charles Wentworth, John Macarthur's son, James, and his nephew, Hannibal Macarthur—all large landowners. Another member was a quarrelsome Scottish clergyman and newspaper proprietor named John Dunmore Lang.

The council now had more power than before. It had the right to propose new laws and to vote on them without the permission of the governor, and the governor was no longer in control of meetings of the council. The governor could still instruct the council to consider new laws, but he could not control how it voted. He was, however, still the most powerful person in the colony. He still had the power to appoint whoever he chose to important positions and to decide how money was to be spent. He could decide what Crown land (land that was not privately owned) was to be sold, and at what price. The Legislative Council was able to impose taxes (known as customs duties) on goods that were imported into the colony, but the governor still had the final say in these and in other financial matters. It was an uneasy sharing of power that, not surprisingly, soon led to bitter conflict.

A meeting of the New South Wales Legislative Council in 1844.

ACHIEVING RESPONSIBLE GOVERNMENT

The governor of New South Wales in 1843, when the colony first elected members of the Legislative Council, was Sir George Gipps. Gipps had arrived in the colony in 1838, at a time when many rich and powerful people in New South Wales were publicly agitating in favour of self-government for the colony. Gipps was destined to clash with many of these people.

Soon after he arrived in New South Wales, Gipps made enemies of many influential people when he decided to cut back the number of convicts that were being used to work on large properties of rich landowners. Gipps believed that the transportation of convicts to the colony should be discontinued. He was convinced that New South Wales would never be ready to govern itself as long as convicts from Britain were still being sent there. When the big landowners could no longer get enough convicts to work on their properties, they suggested that labourers from the Pacific Islands be shipped into the colony to work at very cheap rates. Gipps disagreed with this too. He was strongly opposed to what he considered to be 'slave labour'. So right from the beginning of his time as governor, Gipps made enemies of large landowners, or squatters, as they were called.

When the first members were elected to the newly expanded Legislative Council in 1842, Gipps made it clear that he disapproved of the way the election was carried out, even though he had no control over it. As far as he was concerned, the elected members of the Legislative Council did not really represent most of the people of New South Wales, because only men with money and property could vote. According to Gipps, the Legislative Council represented mainly the interests of rich landowners, such as William Charles Wentworth and the Macarthurs, and not the ordinary people.

Making demands

The dispute between the Gipps and the Legislative Council reached boiling point in April 1844 when Gipps announced new regulations, limiting the amount of land that individual squatters could own to about 50 square kilometres, and imposing a licence fee of 10 pounds per year on each landholding. As many members of the Legislative Council were large landholders, they angrily protested against these regulations. William Charles Wentworth organised a committee of members of the Legislative Council to investigate the disagreements with the governor. This committee finally produced a report which criticised the fact that the governor had the power to make any kinds of laws without the approval of the Legislative Council. The report also pointed out what it claimed was an absurd situation—a colony run by a governor who took his orders from a government on the other side of the world, which had no real knowledge of local conditions. And, of course, any decisions that the British government made about any of the colonies had to be sent in letters by ship, which took months to reach their destination. The report roundly criticised the 'total absence of all responsible government', sarcastically referred to Governor Gipps as a 'mere Imperial officer' who was responsible for 'mischievous policy' and described the state of affairs in the colony as 'a great evil'. In summing up, the report concluded: 'There is but one remedy for these evils—responsible government ... and an absence of all interference on the part of the home [that is, British] authorities.'

The report, perhaps not surprisingly, was not received well in London, and was even criticised by some local people, not for what it said, but for the way it said it. The tone was aggressive and seemed to be an attack on the governor, rather than a reasonable and well-thought-out argument in favour of self-government. An editorial in the *Sydney Morning Herald* blamed William Charles Wentworth for the offensive way in which the demands were made.

While Gipps' clash with the Legislative Council reawakened among many local people the desire for self-government, the report that resulted from it probably ensured that it would not be granted, at least for the time being.

Victoria

Throughout the 1840s, the inhabitants of what was then known as the Port Phillip district, and especially those who lived in the growing town of Melbourne, became increasingly dissatisfied with being part of New South Wales, and the fact that the laws and regulations governing their lives were made in faraway Sydney. They believed that the money being collected from them in taxes and fees on landholdings, as well as money raised from the sale of land, was being spent mainly to improve conditions in Sydney, and that they lived in a neglected part of the colony.

When the new New South Wales Legislative Council was set up in 1842, six of the 24 elected members represented the Port Phillip District. One of them was the forceful Scottish clergyman, John Dunmore Lang.

In 1844, Lang and the other five Port Phillip District representatives wrote a petition to the Queen of England, Queen Victoria, stating that the 'Colonists of Port Phillip are entirely isolated from those of the middle or Sydney District of New South Wales'. It pointed out that 'the community of Port Phillip…already comprises upwards of twenty five thousand souls, and is possessed of two millions of Sheep, one hundred and forty thousand horned cattle, and five thousand horses, besides a very large amount of other valuable property in Vessels, Buildings and cultivated Land', and that in 1843 the district had imported goods worth 183 321 pounds and exported goods to the value of 277 672 pounds. In the light of these and other

Elizabeth Street, Melbourne, in the 1840s.

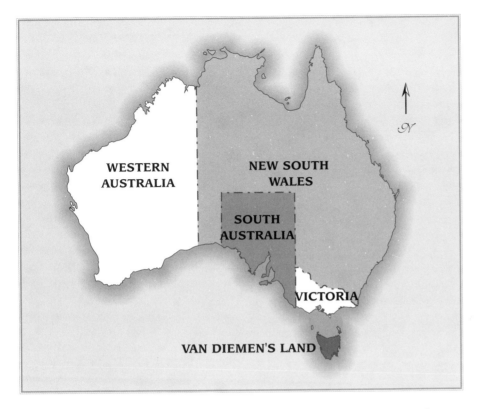

The Australian colonies in 1851, after Victoria separated from New South Wales.

matters, the petitioners argued, the district should be declared a separate colony, completely independent of New South Wales. It was a declaration that reflected the rivalry that already existed between Melbourne and Sydney and that even today remains very strong. This rivalry would later play an important part in the debates to be held towards the end of the century about whether a single nation of Australia was desirable. In the same year, John Dunmore Lang promoted a motion in the New South Wales Legislative Council for separation from New South Wales.

This petition was refused, but the move towards separation from New South Wales grew stronger through the 1840s. Public meetings were held, more petitions were drawn up, and eventually the British government was forced to give the matter serious consideration. A number of inquiries were held and, in August 1850, the British parliament passed the *Australian Colonies' Government Act*, declaring that a new colony of Victoria was to be established in south-eastern Australia, with Melbourne as its capital. A couple of months later, when the news reached Melbourne, there was wild rejoicing in the streets. For a week the city was decorated and lit up at night, salutes of guns were fired, and newspapers published special editions to celebrate the creation of their new colony.

Victoria officially became a separate colony on 1 July 1851.

John Dunmore Lang

Like William Charles Wentworth, John Dunmore Lang was a fighter for the rights, not only of Victoria, but of all the colonies. However, his ideas were even more advanced, for his time, than those of Wentworth. He seemed to have boundless energy: he travelled to and fro between the colonies and England nine times; he founded a weekly newspaper, the *Colonist*, in 1835; and he wrote several books and a huge number of newspaper articles, as well as acting as a Presbyterian minister. He could well be described as a federationist before his time. In 1852 he wrote a book, *Freedom and independence for the golden lands of Australia*, and in 1870 another, titled *The coming event! or freedom and independence for the seven united provinces of Australia*. The event was coming, but not for a long time yet. He even suggested that Australia should be completely independent of Britain and should break off links with the British monarch. In other words, according to Lang, the united Australian colonies should become a 'republic'—a country that does not have a king or queen as its head. In 1870 this was a revolutionary idea.

Getting there

The new Act of the British parliament did more than just declare a new colony. It also spelt out guidelines for how the new colony of Victoria, as well as New South Wales, South Australia and Van Diemen's Land, was to be governed. Western Australia, where convicts were still being sent, would have to wait to get its own parliament. At first, the colonial governments would be modelled on the New South Wales Legislative Council, with two-thirds of their members elected and the councils sharing power, as before, with the governor. However,

John Dunmore Lang.

the rules about who was eligible to vote were made less strict, and a higher proportion of the adult male population of each colony was given the right to vote. It was a small step in the direction of greater democracy. The Act also increased the kinds of laws that the Legislative Councils could make, and looked forward to the time when they would be completely independent. The Act also foreshadowed the creation of a new, separate colony, in the northern part of New South Wales—the colony of Queensland was eventually declared in 1859.

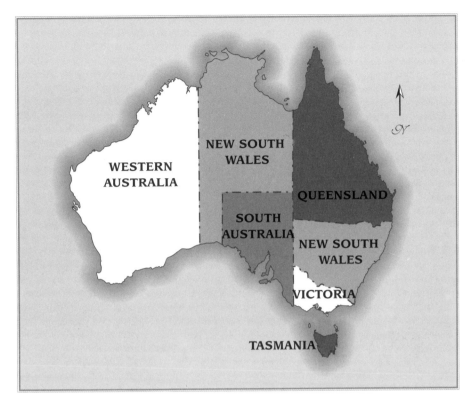

Queensland became a separate colony in 1859.

Gold and government

Early in 1851, gold was discovered at Ophir in central western New South Wales and, not long after, more, and even richer, discoveries were made in the newly declared colony of Victoria. The gold rushes that followed these discoveries dramatically changed the life of both colonies, as people streamed out of the cities to the goldfields and, soon after, even more people flowed into both colonies from all over the world in the quest for a quick fortune. In the following 10 years, the population of New South Wales more than doubled to reach almost 360 000, and that of Victoria increased seven times to almost 540 000. The total population of the Australian colonies in 1861 was more than 1 100 000.

The sudden increase in population and prosperity, as well as the problems that came with them, caused the British government to think again. In 1852, the colonial secretary wrote to the governors of New South Wales, Victoria, Van Diemen's Land and South Australia, saying that because of 'considerations arising from these extraordinary discoveries of Gold', the time had come 'to place full powers of self-government in the hands of a people thus advanced in wealth

and prosperity'. These colonies should, then, the letter went on, draw up new constitutions, setting out rules about how they would be governed. If the British government approved of these constitutions, it would grant these colonies 'responsible government'.

It was not just the effects of the gold rushes that influenced the British government. Early in 1852, the New South Wales Legislative Council, led by William Charles Wentworth, threatened that it would cease to govern the colony if full self-government was not granted. This was no longer a petition; it was a firm demand!

Constitutions and parliaments

The constitutions that were drawn up established the basic pattern on which colonial, and later state, governments would operate. It also set the model which, after federation in 1901, the Australian federal parliament would follow. William Charles Wentworth was appointed by the New South Wales Legislative Council to head a committee to draw up a new constitution for that colony. The other colonies also appointed committees for that purpose.

The opening of the Victorian Legislative Council in 1851.

The constitutions that were drafted came up with similar ideas. They all recommended that, instead of a single Legislative Council, the parliament should have two 'houses'. In New South Wales, the upper house, known as the Legislative Council, was to consist of members who were appointed for life by the governor, and the lower house, the Legislative Assembly, was to be elected by the public. The right to vote was granted to men only, and depended on how much property a person possessed. Some very wealthy people were allowed to have more than one vote. This system varied a little between states, with Victoria, South Australia and Van Diemen's Land, opting to have members of both houses of parliament elected. In South Australia, all white males (Aboriginal people at this stage were not even counted as citizens) over the age of 21 were to have the right to vote for members of the lower house, but the upper house was to be elected only by men of property.

During 1855 and 1856, the British government approved all these constitutions. Responsible government—the right to make laws without the permission of either a governor or the British government—had arrived in the Australian colonies. When Queensland became a separate colony in 1859, it, too, was granted responsible government. Like New South Wales, the members of its upper house, or Legislative Council, were not elected, but were appointed for life. It was not until 1870 that Western Australia, where convicts were still being sent until 1868, had its first elected members of its Legislative Council; and it was only in 1890, at a time when the move towards federation was gathering momentum in the other colonies, that it finally achieved self-government.

EARLY MOVES TOWARDS FEDERATION

In January 1988 there were official celebrations all around Australia. What was being celebrated was what was called Australia's Bicentenary—the 200th anniversary of the arrival of the First Fleet in New South Wales, and the beginning of white settlement on the continent. This marked the start of modern Australia. In 1988 there was no doubt that the people of Australia thought of themselves first and foremost as Australians, whether they lived in Perth in Western Australia, or Cairns in far north Queensland.

Exactly a century earlier, in 1888, there had also been celebrations all over the continent and in Tasmania. In Sydney on 24 January, the premier of New South Wales, Sir Henry Parkes, unveiled a statue of the British queen, Queen Victoria, and two days later, on 26 January, the anniversary of the arrival of the First Fleet in Sydney Cove, he opened Centennial Park in Sydney's east. That evening there was a grand banquet, attended by politicians and other important people. Many poor people were given coupons that they could exchange for food.

Melbourne's Exhibition Building.

Melbourne's 1888 celebrations were held later in the year, in August. There was a huge exhibition of paintings, as well as machinery and inventions, in the grand Exhibition Hall that had been built in Carlton in 1880. There were also concerts of classical music by world-famous musicians, as well as fairground amusements. In small towns throughout the colonies there were picnics, firework displays and processions. Children were given time off from school to watch and take part in these celebrations.

Some of the people who celebrated in 1888 might have called themselves Australians, but the great majority of them still thought of themselves as citizens of Victoria, New South Wales, Queensland, South Australia, Western Australia or Tasmania—one of the six separate colonies of Britain. A country called Australia did not yet exist. Western Australia was still not even a self-governing colony. Canberra, which would later become the capital of the nation, was still a sheep-run in southern New South Wales.

A feeling for nationhood

By 1888, however, the idea of federation had been widely discussed, even though no really positive steps had been taken to achieve it. As early as 1871, an organisation known as the Australian Natives Association had been formed in Melbourne and its members held meetings in which the benefits of federation were discussed. Through the 1880s this organisation became increasingly influential, as its numbers increased from a mere 235 in 1880 to 7400 in 1890. By 1871, six out of every 10 people in the colonies were 'Australian natives'—they were not migrants, but had been born here. By 1888, almost seven out of 10 were Australian-born. As a result, fewer people than before felt a strong loyalty to Britain.

Other factors, too, during the 1880s contributed to a growing feeling that people in different colonies shared many things in common. Sport was one such unifying factor. In 1875, people in all colonies rejoiced when Edward Trickett became the world sculling champion. Then in 1877 an English cricket team played an 'Australian' team (its members were from New South Wales and Victoria) at the Melbourne Cricket Ground, and the colonials won. This is generally considered to be the first 'test' match played between the two countries. In 1882 a combined colonial team defeated England in a series of test matches, thus winning the Ashes, a trophy that English and Australian teams still try to win from each other. These and similar events certainly helped to develop a sense of shared pride.

In 1888, when all the colonies celebrated the birth of the first Australian colony, there were many people who were already enthusiastic about the possibility of federation. At this stage, however, there were probably many more who were indifferent about it or who would have opposed it outright.

The first governor-general

The present constitution of the Commonwealth of Australia states that the British monarch is the head of the Australian nation. However, as the British monarch does not live in Australia and is not closely concerned with Australian matters, he or she is represented in Australia by a person known as the governor-general. Although the governor-general is not involved in making laws, he or she (so far no woman has been governor-general) must sign all laws that the Australian parliament passes on behalf of the British monarch. You read earlier in this book that Lord Hopetoun was the first governor-general of the Commonwealth of Australia. But Hopetoun was not the first person in the Australian colonies to have the title governor-general. That honour goes to Sir Charles FitzRoy, who was governor of New South Wales from 1846 to 1855.

Even in the 1840s, there were some members of the New South Wales Legislative Council who believed that the different Australian colonies could not be completely independent of each other—that there were some areas, such as trade and transport, where the different colonies needed to cooperate with each other and perhaps even have common laws. In 1846, soon after he had arrived in the colony, FitzRoy wrote to Earl Grey, who was then the British colonial secretary, suggesting that somebody in the colony should be given the power to ensure that laws passed in one colony did not conflict with laws in another colony. In other words the different colonies should act together for their common good.

Earl Grey agreed and wrote to FitzRoy in July 1847, suggesting that some 'central authority' should be established 'throughout the whole of the Australian colonies' so that these colonies could cooperate with each other in matters such as 'the imposition of duties of exports and imports, the conveyancing of letters, and the formation of roads [and] railways'. Two years later, Grey went further, suggesting that there should be a person known as a 'governor-general' who would have the power to call a 'general assembly of Australia' if he thought it was necessary. This was the first suggestion of any kind of government for the whole of Australia.

However, this idea proved so unpopular in the colonies that Grey dropped it. In 1851, though, Grey did appoint FitzRoy as 'Governor-General of all Her Majesty's Australian possessions'. In the face of so much opposition in the colonies, however, FitzRoy does not seem to have taken the role of governor-general very seriously and did not attempt to use his powers. For example, in the late 1840s and early 1850s the first railways were built in New South Wales and Victoria. Commonsense should have dictated that the gauge (the width of the lines) in each colony would be the same,

Scenes at an Australia v. England cricket 'test' match in Melbourne in 1882.

as at some stage trains would travel between colonies. But the gauge of train lines built in Victoria was 165 millimetres wider than the gauge in New South Wales. As a result, for almost 100 years after a rail line between Melbourne and Sydney was completed in 1883, passengers travelling between the two capitals had to change trains at Albury, on the New South Wales–Victoria border. FitzRoy, if he wanted to, could probably have insisted that the lines were built to the same gauge, especially as Earl Grey in London often pointed out the absurdity of building lines of different widths. As the different colonies continued to go their own way, the term governor-general was dropped in 1861.

Recommendations

The idea of a federation of all the Australian colonies was eagerly discussed in the 1860s, if not by most people in the colonies, at least by a few people of power and influence. William Charles Wentworth was one of the earliest champions of federation. When he went to present a draft constitution for New South Wales to the British government in 1854, he helped form an organisation called the General Association for the Australian Colonies. Wentworth, backed by members of this organisation, tried to persuade the British government to make laws forcing the different colonies to be part of one nation, but the British government refused.

The opening of the railway line from Sydney to Albury in 1881.

In 1857, committees of both the Victorian and New South Wales parliaments were formed to look at the possibility of federation, and both committees reported in favour of it. They recommended that there should be a conference of leaders of the different colonies to discuss how a national federation could work. However, this conference did not take place, partly because the government of New South Wales refused to agree with what its committee recommended, and partly because the government of South Australia thought that it was too early yet to consider federation.

The Australian politician most in favour of federation at this stage was Charles Gavan Duffy, an Irishman who had stood trial for treason in Britain in 1848, arrived in Victoria in 1855, and was soon after elected to the Victorian Legislative Assembly. He quickly made his mark, introducing laws extending the right to vote in Victoria to all adult white males, regardless of how much property they owned, and also permitting men who did not own property to stand for election to the Victorian Legislative Assembly—both moves towards greater democracy in Victoria. It was Duffy who first suggested the appointment of the 1857 committee in Victoria that recommended federation. He himself was chairman of this committee. When the New South Wales government failed to back his idea for a conference of all the colonies, he angrily blamed it for standing in the way of a united Australian nation.

Duffy was premier of Victoria in 1871–72, but retired from politics in 1880 and went to live in the south of France, where he remained until he died in 1903. When Australia finally achieved federation in 1901, Duffy no doubt rejoiced in the news. However, towards the end of his life, his main interests seem to have been Irish, rather than Australian, politics. He wrote a number of books and many magazine articles, most of them about Irish history.

"UNION IS STRENGTH."

This cartoon, from a Melbourne magazine in 1860, represents Charles Gavan Duffy and his efforts to achieve a united Australian nation.

WHY NO FEDERATION?

During the 1860s and 1870s most people in Australia did not think about federation at all. People who lived in country areas struggling to make a living on small farms, or who worked in factories or offices in the cities, were too busy dealing with day-to-day problems to give much thought, if any, to the idea of nation-building.

You may have heard the phrases 'global village' or 'shrinking world'. The feeling that the world is becoming smaller is a result of advances that have been made, especially in the last few decades, in transport and communications. Today we can pick up a telephone, and speak directly to someone on the other side of the continent, or on the other side of the world. You can travel across Australia in just a few hours, and across the world in less than a day. You can turn on a television and watch a football, cricket, netball or tennis match almost anywhere on earth. You can use email to send instant messages to people all over the globe. A person living in Alice Springs can know what is happening in the Australian parliament in Canberra as quickly as a person who lives and works in Canberra itself.

However, the situation was very different in the 19th century. The phrase 'the tyranny of distance' comes from the name of a book by Geoffrey Blainey, a famous writer about Australian history. The tyranny of distance refers to the problems that the sheer size of the Australian continent created for the people who lived in it during much of the 19th century. The problems were especially great for people who lived in remote country regions or even in small country towns. These towns were often separated from each other by huge stretches of unexplored country. The only news of the outside world that reached these towns and regions in the days before telephones, radio and television was brought by people who travelled to them,

A small, isolated town in Victoria in the mid-19th century.

Travelling along country roads throughout much of the 19th century was difficult, dangerous and slow.

on horseback or by coach, along dusty, boggy and often dangerous roads. They knew little of what was happening in Sydney or Melbourne, and probably cared even less.

Even in Sydney, not much was heard about Melbourne. Until the early 1880s, when a railway joined the two cities, travel between the two cities was difficult. The quickest way to get from one to the other was by steamship—a journey that took about a week.

Under these circumstances, people in one colony felt very distant from those in other colonies, even if they were on the same continent. This was especially true in Western Australia where Perth, on the west coast, was separated by vast stretches of desert from South Australia, the nearest colony to the east. There didn't seem much point in joining forces to create a nation.

Jealousies

Even in the large cities, among wealthy and influential people and those who made the laws, there were many who were against federation, even though they had heard the arguments in favour of it. There were various reasons for this. In Victoria, for example, there was a fear that New South Wales, as the oldest colony, might try to dominate the southern colony. After all, Victoria had struggled throughout the 1840s to separate from New South Wales and was in no hurry to rejoin it. The same was true for Queensland, which had become a separate colony only in 1859. If Victorians were afraid of being dominated by their northern neighbour, New South Wales people had their worries about Victoria, where the gold rushes of the 1850s and 1860s had brought huge population increases and made Melbourne the largest and most prosperous city in the colonies. Again, many people in South Australia looked down on the other colonies because South Australia was settled entirely by people who came there of their own free will and had never had convicts sent there. Again, South Australia, Queensland, Tasmania and Western Australia, which had much smaller populations than New South Wales and Victoria, worried that those two colonies would have almost all the power in a federation and that the interests of the smaller colonies would not be served. All the other colonies, too, resented the fact that in 1850 Western Australia, at the request of its government, started accepting convicts from Britain. By this time the transportation of convicts had ceased in all the colonies except Tasmania, where the last convicts arrived in 1853. Convicts continued to be sent to Western Australia until 1868.

SHRINKING THE CONTINENT

The first steam railway in the Australian colonies began to operate in Victoria in September 1854. It ran between Melbourne and Port Melbourne. The following year a railway between Sydney and Parramatta was opened in New South Wales. From these beginnings the railways expanded quickly. By 1861 there were almost 400 kilometres of railway tracks in New South Wales, Victoria and South Australia. Twenty years later, there were more than 6500 kilometres of tracks, and steam trains were running in all Australian colonies. By the time of federation in 1901, the capital cities of the three eastern colonies and South Australia were linked by rail, and railways covered a total distance of almost 40 000 kilometres. Only Western Australia remained isolated—its rail link to Adelaide was not completed until 1917.

The 'iron horse', as the railways were often called, also had a significant effect on people's attitudes to the land they lived in. Newspapers hailed the new means of transport as a sign that the colonies were coming of age and could take their place as part of the modern, civilised world. The railways were even portrayed as bringing 'civilisation' to country areas, putting them in touch with the life of the cities. More importantly, though, the railways seemed to bring the colonies closer together, helping to reduce the tyranny of distance that you read

Scenes from the celebrations at the opening of Victorian Railways on 14 June 1883, completing the link between Melbourne and Sydney.

about on page 32. Even before it was possible to travel by train between one colony and another, there was talk of how the railway would unify the country.

A new wonder

The opening of a new railway line was a big event in the Australian colonies in the 19th century. The new trains, with their noisy steam-powered locomotives, brought people flocking in their thousands to see and wonder at them. These early trains, with their rough wooden carriages pulled by primitive-looking steam engines, to us would appear crude and uncomfortable, but to the people of 150 years ago, they were wonders of modern engineering and technology. Often the opening of a new railway line would bring together brass bands, choirs and a host of dignitaries who would take the opportunity to make grand and lengthy speeches to the assembled crowd.

When a railway line was opened between Melbourne and Beechworth in 1876, the premier of Victoria told the large crowd that attended the opening that the railways would soon be responsible for bringing the country together under a single government. When the railway line linking Sydney with Albury, near the Victorian border, was opened in 1881, the premier of New South Wales, Sir Henry Parkes, and the premier of Victoria, Graham Berry, were among the speakers. Parkes could not resist the temptation to make comparisons between the two colonies—he claimed that New South Wales was forward-looking and adventurous, while Victorians were mainly interested in competing against each other. Nevertheless, Parkes predicted that these two colonies would soon lead the way in creating 'one great united Australia'.

This united country did not eventuate as quickly as Parkes would have liked—he did not live to see federation achieved—but by 1881 the railways, along with the improvements in communication, had helped to create a momentum towards unifying the country under one government.

A steam train crosses the Flinders Ranges in inland South Australia in the early 1880s.

Explorers

Right throughout the 19th century, explorers pushed further and further into parts of the Australian continent where white people had never been before, gradually solving the mysteries of what this vast country was really like. By the 1860s most of the questions about what lay beyond the settled areas had been answered. As newspapers reported the often heroic feats of the explorers, people gradually grew to understand the nature of the huge landmass that all of them, except Tasmanians, shared. They realised that the great majority of them lived around the fertile edges of a dry and harsh, but endlessly fascinating, country. With this knowledge came a growing sense that while they belonged to a particular colony, that colony was part of something larger.

Two of the great achievements of Australian exploration occurred in the early 1860s and created widespread public interest and excitement. At the beginning of March 1860, a party

McDouall Stuart reaches the centre of the continent.

two-thirds of the distance. The Burke and Wills expedition did succeed in reaching the northern coast, but both Burke and Wills had died in the desert on the way back and four other members of the team had also perished on the journey. The tragedy of Burke and Wills quickly established itself in people's minds as a great national legend, something that belonged, not only to Victoria, but to the whole of Australia.

The Overland Telegraph

McDouall Stuart, too, soon achieved the status of a national, as well as a South Australian, hero when in January 1863, he rode into Adelaide, broken in health, after finally succeeding in crossing the continent from the south to a point near Palmerston (which was later called Darwin) and then back again. Stuart's successful crossing had blazed the way for another great achievement—the building of the Overland Telegraph Line between Darwin and Port Augusta in South Australia between 1870 and 1872. This consisted of single electric wire strung out across the continent between telegraph poles, and was a huge feat of construction and engineering. It followed fairly closely the route that Stuart and his party had mapped out on their successful crossing. When it was completed, Charles Todd, the postmaster-general of South Australia, who supervised the construction of this line, called it a 'grand electric chain' through which 'the Australian colonies were connected'. It also connected the Australian colonies to the rest of the world, because it was joined by an underwater cable to the island of Java, now part of Indonesia, from where it linked into telegraph networks that stretched through Asia and to Europe.

The first electric telegraph in the colonies was introduced into Victoria in 1854. Four years later, Melbourne, Sydney and Adelaide were linked by telegraph and, in 1859, an underwater cable linked Tasmania into this network.

led by John McDouall Stuart set out from a place north of Adelaide in South Australia in the first ever attempt to go right across the continent from south to north. The South Australian government had offered 2000 pounds to the first expedition to achieve this feat. Almost six months later, on 20 August 1860, an expedition led by John O'Hara Burke, and including William John Wills, was given a hero's send-off when it set out from Melbourne, also bound for the top end of the continent. Newspapers depicted the two expeditions as a race, almost like a great sporting event between two rival colonies. But these attempts were keenly followed by people in all the colonies, especially in the cities, where newspapers speculated on the progress of the expeditions and reported news when it came to hand.

In both cases, the news was bad. Stuart's team had to turn back after covering about

In 1861 telegraph lines were extended to Brisbane. The Overland Telegraph Line, therefore, meant that all the colonies, except Western Australia, could now communicate by telegraph with Britain. Messages that took weeks to arrive before this time, could now be sent in a few hours. At a ceremony to celebrate the completion of the Overland Telegraph Line, Henry Parkes, who had recently become premier of New South Wales, spoke of the 'magical work' which now united 'us hand in hand with the mother country'. In 1877, 36 years after another explorer, Edward John Eyre, had forged an overland route between South Australia and the west coast of the continent, a telegraph line from Adelaide to Perth was completed, and Western Australia was now connected to the rest of Australia and the rest of the world.

The telegraph, and particularly the Overland Telegraph Line, was an important step in bringing the colonies closer together. Yet another step was not long in arriving. In 1880 the first telephone services were introduced, first in Melbourne, and soon after in Sydney and Brisbane. Telephone services came to Adelaide and Hobart in 1883 and finally to Perth in 1887. A telephone link between Melbourne and Sydney was established in 1884. Even though the private telephone was still a thing of the future—it would be another 50 years before telephones were installed in many Australian homes—the coming of telephones, hard on the heels of the telegraph services, meant that Australians could sense that the tyranny of distance, and the feeling of isolation that went with it, were slowly being conquered.

A ceremony in Palmerston to mark the beginning of work on the Overland Telegraph Line in 1870.

CONFERENCES

As we saw on page 33, one of the reasons that early suggestions for a federation of all the colonies fell mainly on deaf ears was that colonies such as Victoria and Queensland, which had only recently separated from New South Wales and were now governing themselves, were not keen to give up their independence. As well, the smaller colonies feared that any government that had control over all the colonies would be dominated by New South Wales and Victoria, where most of the Australian population lived. As we also saw, there was strong rivalry between New South Wales and Victoria, and even though this was often expressed in a light-hearted way, it was still deeply felt. Melbourne and Sydney were especially jealous of each other. Both cities were expanding quickly and their citizens liked to think of themselves as living in the greatest and most prosperous city in the colonies. In the 1860s and 1870s, then, Australians in different parts of the continent were far from ready to think seriously about joining forces. They could not even agree on something as obviously sensible as building their railway tracks the same width!

The tariff problem

However, just as neighbours in a street have to agree to cooperate about things that concern them all, even if they sometimes may disagree and quarrel with each other, so the different Australian colonies were forced by circumstances to discuss and come to some agreements about certain matters that were important to them all.

In 1856, the first of a series of 'intercolonial conferences', as they became known, was held in Melbourne. This one was called to discuss the building and maintenance of lighthouses around the coastline for the protection of ships that visited and brought goods to ports in each of the different colonies.

The goods that were carried on ships, on river barges or on wagons that travelled between the colonies were one of the main subjects discussed at another intercolonial conference, again held in Melbourne, in 1863. The governor of South Australia, Sir Dominick Daly, had suggested that this conference be

A lighthouse on Sydney Harbour in 1880, built to protect ships bringing in goods from other colonies.

held mainly in order to discuss the question of tariffs. A tariff, or 'customs duty', is a tax that a government charges on goods coming into a country'. One reason for tariffs is to protect certain industries within a country against competition from cheaper goods that come in from other countries. For example, the Australian government charges a tariff on motor vehicles imported from other countries. This makes the price of these cars dearer than they would have been if there were no tariff, and encourages people to buy cars that are manufactured in Australia.

Today, there is no tariff on goods taken between different parts of Australia, but in colonial times the different colonies did charge tariffs on many goods that travelled between them. The main problem with this was that different colonies charged tariffs on different goods and also charged different rates of tariff. You can imagine how complicated this made trade between the colonies and how confusing the situation was. For one thing, it meant that at various places along the borders between the colonies, customs houses had to be set up in order to inspect goods and collect any tariffs that needed to be paid. The sensible thing would have been to have all the colonies agree to the same level of tariffs—in other words, to impose 'uniform' tariff laws—or to do away with tariffs altogether—that is, to allow 'free trade' between the colonies.

The problem was that the individual colonies were very jealous of the tariffs they collected and were afraid that if uniform tariffs were brought in they might lose some of the money they were collecting. The difficulty of getting any agreement on these matters is shown by the fact that neither Queensland or Western Australia even attended the 1863 conference. The reply from Queensland to the invitation stated that it was not prepared to agree to any 'arrangement' that may force it to 'sacrifice a considerable portion of our Customs revenue'.

The other four colonies each sent three delegates to the 1863 intercolonial conference.

One of the things they agreed upon was that there should be uniform tariffs. But the conference had no power to force the governments of individual colonies to follow its advice. All it could do was 'urge' the governments to do so. As things turned out, governments continued to charge different rates on different goods and the tariff problem remained unresolved.

A continuing problem

The same question was considered at another intercolonial conference, held in Melbourne in 1870. Once again, no delegates from Queensland or Western Australia attended. At this conference there was disagreement between New South Wales and Victoria and, as in 1863, there was no progress towards achieving uniform tariff laws.

The fact that the colonies could not agree among themselves about tariff laws was probably a major factor in delaying the arrival of federation for another 30 years after the 1870 intercolonial conference. It symbolised the jealousies and the distrust that existed between them. However, the very fact that these tariff laws did not work very well was eventually an important factor in making people realise that working together was better than working against each other, and in creating a climate of cooperation that allowed federation to take place. Right to the bitter end, however, the question of uniform tariffs was being used as an argument, especially in the smaller colonies, that federation would put individual colonies at a disadvantage.

As the colonies grew in population and prosperity, trade with foreign countries became increasingly important. But foreign countries found it very difficult to understand the different tariff laws that applied among the Australian colonies. Finally it dawned on governments and people who wanted to trade their goods that these differing tariff laws were a creating a barrier to good trade arrangements and were working to the disadvantage of all colonies and to the advantage of none. But this took a long time to happen.

The value of intercolonial conferences

The two intercolonial conferences discussed above both dealt mainly with the problems of trade between the colonies and both failed to bring about any major change in this area. But the 1863 conference had more than just tariffs to consider. Among other items on its agenda were: transportation of convicts; improving the inland rivers of the continent, such as the Murray and the Darling, so that they could be used for transport and irrigation; the maintenance of lighthouses; arrangements about postal services between the colonies; and encouraging more migrants to come to the Australian colonies from Britain. Other intercolonial conferences, held in the 1860s, 1870s and early 1880s, dealt with a range of issues, including postal services, communications and immigration. Some of them led to agreements between the colonies. Often, however, the delegates who attended the conferences were unable to persuade, or 'urge', their governments to do what the conferences had suggested. However, one subject on which the governments did agree with the conferences' suggestions was immigration. They agreed that people from Britain should be encouraged to come to the colonies, but that people from China and other parts of Asia or the Pacific Islands, or from Africa, should be refused entry. This policy, which was known as the White Australia Policy, and which most Australians now consider to be racist, was the policy of Australian governments right up to the 1960s.

The last intercolonial conference was in Sydney in 1883. Many people felt that these conferences had been a failure. James Service, who became premier of Victoria in 1883, summed up the general dissatisfaction with them when he said: 'The outcome of the whole of these conferences has really not been worth the time and trouble they cost...I hold in my hand a list of subjects dealt with by intercolonial conferences...There are some twenty three of them altogether, and if I say about three subjects have been

'Kanakas' were brought from the Pacific Islands to Queensland to work on farms and sugar plantations.

dealt with effectively by these conferences I think I state the full number.' Clearly a more effective way of dealing with problems that all the colonies shared needed to be found.

Intercolonial tensions

One important matter on which all the delegates to the 1863 intercolonial conference agreed was about transportation of convicts. The delegates at the 1863 intercolonial conference all agreed that that no more convicts should be sent to any of the colonies. In the formal and rather stiff language that was used in such documents, the report on the conference resolved that: 'this Conference address Her Most Gracious Majesty the Queen, praying that Transportation may not be established or continued in any portion of Her Majesty's Australian Dependencies'. At this stage, only Western Australia was still receiving convicts—they continued to be sent there until 1868. The fact that Western Australia was still accepting convicts from Britain was a cause of conflict and tension between it and the other Australian colonies. It was a factor that added to the sense of isolation that many West Australians felt then, and that almost resulted in Western Australia not joining with the other colonies when they eventually federated in 1901.

On the question of immigration of non-white people, there was also strong disagreement between Queensland and the other colonies. From the 1860s until early in the 20th century, Queensland farmers had been shipping in people from the Pacific Islands, mainly the New Hebrides (now Vanuatu) and the Solomon Islands, to work, first on farms or cattle and sheep stations, and later on sugar plantations. Many Queenslanders thought that these people, who were used to tropical conditions, were better able than white people to work in the Queensland heat. The real reason, however, was that they could be employed for only a fraction of the cost of hiring white people. More than 60 000 of these islanders, who were called 'Kanakas', came to Queensland. Sometimes they were brought there against their will, and in many cases they were forced to work in appalling conditions. The practice was widely condemned in New South Wales and other colonies and proved an ongoing source of tension between the northern colony and its southern neighbours—yet another factor that helped to separate the colonies and to delay attempts at federation.

Labour vessel landing Kanakas in Queensland.

CONCERNS ABOUT DEFENCE

In 1854 war broke out between Russia, on one side, and Britain, France and Turkey on the other. Turkey was still a powerful country then and, like Britain, had a large empire. It was known as the Ottoman Empire. Russia was attempting to take possession of parts of this empire, and Britain and France went to war to prevent this. This war, known as the Crimean War, lasted until 1856. It frightened a lot of people in the Australian colonies. They feared that, as an enemy of Britain, Russia might send its warships into the Pacific to attack British colonies there. As a result, in 1855, New South Wales built a warship of its own. It was named the *Spitfire*. The following year, Victoria acquired the *Victoria*, which would defend Port Phillip Bay and Melbourne against any attack. New South Wales, Victoria and South Australia also formed small armies of their own at this time. Until now, people in the colonies had not felt threatened by foreign nations and had not been particularly concerned about matters of defence. They were confident they could rely on Britain to defend them if necessary.

As the colonies grew and developed, the British government encouraged them to take more responsibility for their own defence. Eventually, in 1870, Britain withdrew all its armed forces from the Australian colonies, although it continued to provide ships for naval protection until well after federation. Ships belonging to the colonies joined with British ships to form what became known as the 'Royal Navy's Australian Squadron'.

The withdrawal of British troops caused many people to think seriously about how the colonies could defend themselves if they were attacked. Six colonies with six small armies, all independent of each other, did not seem a very sensible way to defend a huge continent. Even as early as the 1850s, it had been seriously suggested that the need to defend the colonies

The Victoria *was launched in 1855 to defend Port Phillip Bay.*

Sir Thomas McIlwraith.

Dutch had also taken control of the western side of New Guinea. The Australian colonies had, then, lived with a Dutch presence to their north for a long time. They did not think that this posed any real threat to their security.

It was different, however, when, in the 1870s and early 1880s, German traders arrived and established themselves in the northeastern part of New Guinea and the nearby smaller islands. People in the colonies became increasingly concerned about a possible threat from the north. This concern turned to alarm in early 1883, when a German ship bound for New Guinea sailed into Sydney to gather supplies. Almost immediately, Sir Thomas McIlwraith, the premier of Queensland, the colony closest to New Guinea, declared the southern part of New Guinea to be a British territory. He even sent a ship to the settlement of Port Moresby in New Guinea to raise the British flag there. McIlwraith fully expected the British government to support him in this move and was both surprised and angered when it sent a message refusing to back up his action. At this stage, Britain believed that Germany had no interest in occupying part of New Guinea. And Britain certainly did not want to start a quarrel with this powerful European country.

was a strong argument in favour of joining together as a single nation. However the question of a single defence force was not really taken very seriously before the 1880s. Although individual colonies continued to maintain armed forces, these declined greatly during the 1870s, when there did not seem to be any real threat to the colonies' security.

New Guinea

New Guinea is a large island directly to the north of Australia, separated from the northern tip of Queensland only by the narrow stretch of water known as Torres Strait. For more than two centuries the Dutch had controlled the islands that now make up the Republic of Indonesia, to the north and northwest of the Australian continent. This region was then known as the Dutch East Indies. In 1828 the

Ships of the Royal Navy's Australian Squadron, 1881.

As we saw on page 41, Queensland had serious disagreements with the other colonies about the use of Pacific Islanders on its farms, pastoral properties and sugar plantations. Some of these labourers had come from New Guinea and the smaller islands off its coasts, where Germany now seemed to be about to take control. Despite these disagreements, however, all the colonies now acted together and supported the Queensland premier's actions. They all condemned Britain for what they saw as its cowardice. A couple of colonies even suggested sending boats and troops to conquer various Pacific Islands to keep foreign countries away from them. The Queensland government immediately put in an order for two new gunboats.

New Caledonia

Yet another cause for alarm was the presence of the French in the Pacific region. France had established a colony in New Caledonia and had been sending convicts there since 1864. Many people in Australia feared that the French had their eyes on the islands of the New Hebrides, to the west of New Caledonia, and wanted to expand further in the Pacific. The New Hebrides are now the islands of Vanuatu. Many colonists were also concerned that dangerous French convicts could escape from New Caledonia and make their way to the eastern coast of Australia. In fact, a few convicts from the French colony had already reached Australian shores. The premier of Victoria, James Service, was so worried about French ambitions in the region that he sent a series of telegraph messages to the British government, demanding that it annex the New Hebrides—that is, that it declare those islands to be a British possession.

An intercolonial conference was promptly called to discuss these possible threats to the Australian colonies. This, the last of the intercolonial conferences, was held in Sydney in November 1883.

In 1883, the Basilisk, *was sent from Queensland to explore parts of the New Guinea coast.*

A FEDERAL COUNCIL

So great was the concern about the presence of Germany and France in the Pacific region that not only all the Australian colonies, but New Zealand and Fiji, which were also British colonies, sent delegates to the intercolonial conference that began in Sydney in November 1883. At this stage, some people who supported the idea of the Australian colonies coming together in a federation thought that New Zealand and Fiji should also be part of this federation—in other words they supported the idea of an 'Australasian', rather than a purely Australian, federation. Before the 1883 conference a number of 'residents of the Crown Colony of Fiji' drew up a petition stating that they regarded 'the question of the ultimate Federation of the Australasian Colonies as one of vital importance to the interests of this colony'. However, given the attitude of colonial Australians to non-white peoples (see page 40), it is unlikely that Fiji and Australia could ever have become part of a single nation. Union with New Zealand, on the other hand, might have been possible—Sir Henry Parkes certainly considered that the two countries should be joined as one—except for the fear held by New Zealanders that they would be dominated by Australia, and the fact that New Zealand was separated from the Australian colonies by almost 2000 kilometres of ocean.

At the conference, Sir Samuel Griffith, who had now replaced Sir Thomas McIlwraith as premier of Queensland, suggested that a 'Federal Council of Australasia' be set up, mainly so that the colonies could act together in matters relating to defence, but also so that they could cooperate in 'other matters of general Australasian interest'. The question of federation was raised and discussed at the conference, but the delegates agreed 'that the time has not yet arrived at which a complete federal union of the Australasian Colonies can be attained'. However, delegates also agreed that 'there are many matters of general interest with respect to which united action would be advantageous'.

The conference resolved, then, that the Federal Council would be formed and that it would meet at least every two years. Each self-governing colony would send two representatives to the council's meetings, and Western Australia and Fiji, which had not yet achieved responsible government (they were known as 'Crown' colonies), would each send one. The council would have the power to make laws, but only about matters relating to defence and to relations with other countries. It would have no power to consider questions such as tariffs, which, as we have seen, were creating serious tensions between different colonies. Even so, it looked as though a real step in the direction of an Australian, or even an Australasian, federation had been taken.

Insults, delays and other problems

Before the Federal Council could be set up officially, the British parliament in London had to approve it. This probably would have happened quite quickly if all the Australasian colonies had been able to agree. Although all the delegates to the 1883 conference had agreed to Sir Samuel Griffith's resolution, the governments of some of the colonies did not. South Australia and New Zealand decided not to join the council and, most serious of all, so did New South Wales.

Almost as soon as the conference in Sydney had finished, serious rivalry had flared up between New South Wales and Victoria and insults were exchanged. At a banquet in Melbourne, held just after the conference, the Victorian premier, James Service, accused one of the New South Wales delegates, Sir John Robertson, of treating Victoria and Queensland like 'children' who had 'run away from the mother colony'. He claimed that he had found the people of Sydney 'ignorant' and intensely jealous of 'Melbourne and the Melbourne

James Service.

people'. In fact, it was true that, although they voted in favour of forming the Federal Council, the New South Wales representatives at the conference had not shown themselves particularly enthusiastic about it. In response to Service's attack, a member of the New South Wales parliament referred to James Service sarcastically as a 'champion of federation' who had 'spoken more bunkum on the subject than any 20 men in Australia'. Sir John Robertson then compounded his insult to Victoria by referring to that colony as no more than a 'cabbage garden'. Then another member of the New South Wales parliament claimed that New South Wales was as far above Victoria as heaven was above earth.

Also, there was a feeling in New South Wales that Victoria would try to dominate the new Federal Council. The result of all this was that the New South Wales parliament voted not to join the Federal Council. Without New South Wales, the British government wondered whether there was any point in agreeing to the council being formed. It was almost two years before Britain gave its approval and it was not until January 1886 that the first meeting of the council took place. This happened in Hobart, with representatives from Western Australia, Queensland, Victoria, Tasmania and Fiji. South Australia did join the council in 1888, but left it again in 1890. New South Wales never joined. The council continued meeting until 1899, but never amounted to much more than a debating society.

Given all the bitterness that it stirred up, the formation of the Federal Council was probably more of a stumbling block in the way of federation than a positive move towards achieving it.

New developments

By the time the Federal Council met for the first time, one of the main reasons for forming it—the problem of German activity in north New Guinea—no longer really existed. In early 1844, Germany sent soldiers to occupy part of northern New Guinea, giving it the name of Kaiser Wilhelm Land. The British government then had to face the fact that it had made a mistake. It hastily sent a ship to Port Moresby to raise the British flag there and declare the southern part of New Guinea, the part known as Papua, to be a British possession. With the British established between them and the Germans, the colonists now felt safer, if not completely satisfied.

In the early 1880s, too, France ceased sending its most dangerous criminals to its colony in New Caledonia, and in 1887 France and Britain reached an agreement to jointly administer the New Hebrides. Once again, the worst fears of Australians about French ambitions in the Pacific were not realised. The concerns about defence, which had prompted the formation of the Federal Council, were now largely resolved.

THE 'FATHER OF FEDERATION'

Henry Parkes must have looked on with great frustration as the Federal Conference, which his colony of New South Wales had refused to join, failed to make any progress towards federation. After all, it was Parkes who, at an intercolonial conference held in Sydney in 1881, had first suggested the idea of a Federal Council that could be the first move towards an eventual federation of the colonies. In proposing this council, Parkes had suggested that such a council would be 'an organisation which would lead men to think in the direction of Federation, and accustom the public mind to federal ideas [and] would be the best preparation for the foundation of Federal Government'. When, however, the individual colonial governments considered this proposal, only three colonies —New South Wales, South Australia and Tasmania— voted in favour of it. As a result, nothing came of it for the time being.

In 1881, Parkes was in the middle of his third term as premier of New South Wales and was now 66 years of age. He was thinking of retiring from politics and must have seen his ambition of bringing about a federation of Australian colonies as slipping further away than ever. Since the 1850s, Parkes had been an ardent supporter of the idea of federation and would have seen its achievement as the crowning glory of a long, brilliant, but often difficult and distressing, career, in which he had come from being the uneducated son of poor English tenant farmers to one of the most powerful men in the Australian colonies.

Sir Henry Parkes at his home in Faulconbridge, New South Wales.

In 1823, when Henry was only eight years old, Parkes' father was forced to leave his farm in Warwickshire in England because he could not pay his debts. The family moved to the industrial city of Birmingham, where the young Henry became an apprentice to a bone and ivory turner. At the age of 21 he married Clarinda Varney and tried to set up his own ivory business in Birmingham. When this failed, the young couple moved to London, where Parkes again tried, and failed, to establish himself in business.

The move to New South Wales

In 1839 Parkes and his wife emigrated to try their fortunes in New South Wales. They came under an assisted immigration scheme which was set up to attract free settlers to the colonies. The Parkes' lives were difficult at this stage. Not only had they failed in business, but two children that had been born to them had died. In New South Wales, Parkes worked first as a farm labourer, and then as a customs officer. In 1845 he started his own ivory business in Sydney. He soon became involved with people interested in politics, and in 1850 he was prominent in opposing a British plan to resume the transportation of convicts to New South Wales. In the same year he set up and edited a newspaper, the *Empire*, in which he often criticised the opinions of prominent people whose ideas he disagreed with. He severely criticised some parts of the draft constitution that William Charles Wentworth had drawn up for New South Wales, even though both men shared similar ideas about a federation of the Australian colonies. Through the *Empire*, Parkes strongly promoted his support for an Australian federation.

In 1854, Parkes was elected to the New South Wales parliament. But he resigned two years later because his newspaper was losing money badly. In 1858, Parkes was unable to pay his debts, and suffered the humiliation of being declared bankrupt. As a result the *Empire* ceased publication. Despite this, he was once again elected the following year as a member of the New South Wales Legislative Assembly. In 1870 Parkes was again publicly disgraced when he was declared bankrupt for the second time, this time with debts much greater than those he had in 1858. Once again he bounced back from the brink of ruin. He was elected again to the Legislative Assembly in 1871 and the following year became premier of New South Wales.

Committed to federation

Henry Parkes was a very dominating personality. He did not take kindly to people who disagreed with him and often tried to bully people into accepting his opinions. As his pictures show, he was also an impressive-looking figure, especially in later life, with his huge white beard, flowing silver hair and hard, staring gaze. He was almost impossible to mistake in any of the many group photographs in which he appeared. As well as being a commanding presence, Parkes was also a powerful public speaker, even if his enemies often made fun of his rough, uneducated accent and the fact that he had a habit of 'dropping his h's'.

Although Parkes retired from parliament in 1884, just before he turned 70, he could not stay away for long, and the next year he was again elected to the New South Wales Legislative Assembly. He became premier again in 1887 and yet again from 1889 to 1891. It was during this last period as premier that he made his greatest contribution to the cause of federation. This ambitious man knew by now that time for him was running out.

Defence again

By the late 1880s the British government had become concerned about the state of defences in the Australian colonies. Only the few ships of the Royal Navy's Australian Squadron and the six separate armies of the individual colonies were there to defend Australia against any possible invasion. In 1889, Major-General James Bevan Edwards, the commander of the British forces in China, arrived in Australia to write a report to the British government about the state of colonial defences. In his report,

Sir Henry Parkes in his office in Sydney in 1891.

Edwards stated his belief that other countries, especially China and other Asian nations, would see Australia as a 'rich prize' that, unless its defences were greatly improved, could quite easily be overrun. He strongly urged that the colonies should all combine to form a single army under a single commander—in other words, they should form a military federation. This, of course, left open the question: if there was only one army for all the colonies, which government would control this army? It seemed logical to Edwards, and to Parkes, that if six colonies shared a single army, then they should also share a single government.

When Parkes telegraphed the premier of Victoria, who was now Duncan Gillies, suggesting that they should consult about the possibility of forming a federation, Gillies replied that the Federal Council was the most suitable place for such a discussion. Parkes knew that the Federal Council was now a weak organisation that had failed to achieve any progress—and, in any case, New South Wales was not a member of it and was not about to back down and join now. Parkes decided to act on his own.

The Tenterfield address

Tenterfield is a small town in the north-east of New South Wales, just south of the border with Queensland. Travelling on the newly opened railway line linking Sydney and Brisbane, Parkes stopped off at Tenterfield on the evening of 24 October 1889 to attend a banquet at the school of arts building there. Parkes was a well-known and popular figure in the area as he had represented the region in the New South Wales parliament from 1882 to 1884. After dinner, Parkes made a speech that many people regard as the real starting point of the push to federation that gathered momentum over the following decade.

In an impassioned address that was frequently applauded by his audience, Parkes outlined the views expressed by 'General Edwards', and then posed the 'great question …whether the time had not now come for the creation on this Australian continent of an Australian Government, as distinct from local Governments now in existence'. He pointed out that, with a population of three and a half million people, Australia had about the same population as the United States did when it went to war with Britain and gained its independence just over 100 years earlier. He was loudly cheered when he claimed that 'surely what the Americans had done by war, the Australians could bring about in peace, without breaking the ties that held them to the mother country'. The only argument against such an idea, he said, could be that the colonies were not yet ready to unite— that the time had not yet come. But, he asserted, and he was applauded as he said it, the time *had* come, and there was no reason for further delay.

Another conference

Fired up with enthusiasm, the 74-year-old Parkes sent telegraph messages to the premiers of the other colonies, including New Zealand, suggesting a special conference to discuss federation. Some were reluctant to come, but all finally agreed. Australia's ability to defend itself became the issue that fuelled the slow but growing progress towards federation.

In February 1890, representatives of all the Australian colonies met in Melbourne, not to draw up definite plans for federation, but merely to discuss whether the time was right to start doing so. Parkes dominated the proceedings and eloquently addressed the gathering. He conjured up the idea of Australia as a nation 'not behind any nation in the world' in either skill 'or in the higher refinements of civilised society'. He spoke of the 'crimson thread of kinship' which united all Australians and looked back to the time 'not so long ago…when I arrived here', before Victoria and Queensland had separated, when the great majority of Australians lived in the one colony of New South Wales. He also looked back to more recent events, saying, 'I have no doubt whatever in my mind that if there had been a central government in Australia—if Australia could have spoken with one voice in the year 1883, New Guinea would have belonged to Australia'.

Parkes' arguments carried the day, although some delegates expressed doubts. The Victorian premier, Duncan Gillies, talked of the tariff problem as the 'lion' which could still stand in the way of a federated Australia, while Sir John Hall, from New Zealand, raised the 'tyranny of distance' question, saying that every mile that separated New Zealand from Australia represented a reason that they could not unite as a country.

The 1890 conference was a triumph for Parkes and for the push towards federation. Although it was an 'informal' meeting with no power to make binding decisions, it paved the way for a 'National Australasian Convention' to be held just over a year later in Sydney. This convention would produce the first draft of a constitution for the nation of Australia.

Delegates to the Melbourne conference in February 1890.

DRAFTING A CONSTITUTION

Despite the success of the Melbourne conference, things were not going well for Sir Henry Parkes in 1890, and they were about to get worse. Parkes had always lived extravagantly and beyond his means. In 1890 he was desperately short of money and unable to pay his debts. He relied on money from his supporters to maintain his lifestyle. He was also now in poor health and was advised by his doctor that his heart was weak. He was a larger-than-life figure who made many enemies. He was often ridiculed in newspaper cartoons. His personal behaviour and morals were often attacked. He had shocked many people when, in February 1889, less than a year after his first wife had

died, he had married a woman 40 years younger than he was. And in May 1890 he was lucky to survive an accident when a carriage he was travelling in through Sydney rolled over. He broke his leg in two places.

In March 1891, however, he was well enough to attend the National Australasian Convention, where 45 delegates—seven from each of the Australian colonies and three from New Zealand—gathered to try to find a formula for federation. Parkes was elected president of this convention and he presented the delegates with a list of proposals about how the new nation should be governed. Included among them were proposals for: a single army and

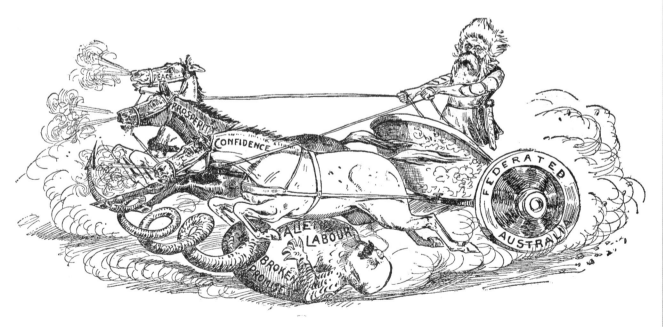

SATURDAY EVENING. JULY 20, 1895.

Vote for SIR HENRY PARKES,
Federation, Local Government, and General Prosperity.

TRIUMPHANT RETURN OF SIR HENRY PARKES.

Parkes shown as a Roman charioteer, riding towards federation over his enemy George Reid.

navy to be under the control of the national government; free trade between the states—which would replace the word 'colonies'; and the right of each state to make its own laws, except in matters that affected the whole country. He also suggested that the national government should consist of two houses of parliament, to be known as the House of Representatives and the Senate. The Senate would have the power to review laws made by the House of Representatives, but could not make laws on its own. Parkes also proposed that the new nation be known as the Commonwealth of Australia. In a rousing speech to the convention, Parkes used the phrase that would become a rallying call for federation throughout the rest of the decade: 'One nation, one destiny.'

Alfred Deakin.

A first draft

The convention lasted for six weeks, and at the end of it many delegates felt confident that federation would very soon be achieved. They had agreed to a draft constitution that in many ways laid down the principles according to which Australia would later be governed. The work of drawing up this constitution was given to four delegates, all of them lawyers, and all of them, except Griffith, born in the colonies: Sir Samuel Griffith from Queensland, Andrew Inglis Clark from Tasmania, Charles Cameron Kingston from South Australia and Edmund Barton from New South Wales.

Much of the work on this draft constitution was done on the Hawkesbury River, north of Sydney, aboard the *Lucinda*, a steamship on which Griffith had travelled to the convention from Queensland. Griffith was the main contributor to this early attempt at a constitution.

One of the things he strongly believed was that the Senate (the upper house of the new Australian parliament) should have an equal number of members from each of the states, no matter how large their populations. This would help to ensure that the interests of the smaller states would be protected if the larger states, such as New South Wales and Victoria, tried to act against them. This provision was written into the draft constitution and became a key feature of the constitution that was finally adopted at the end of the century.

Another important delegate to this convention was Alfred Deakin, a lawyer from Victoria who would later be prime minister of Australia three times between 1903 and 1910. It was mainly Deakin who convinced wavering delegates that the term 'Commonwealth of Australia' should be adopted and, more significantly, that delegates to future federation conventions should be elected by the people and not merely appointed by governments of the different colonies. Deakin sensed that federation could only be achieved if the ordinary people believed in it and felt they were involved.

The two men who, during the 1890s, probably did more than any others to promote federation were the men who would be the first and second prime ministers of the new nation: Edmund Barton from New South Wales and Alfred Deakin from Victoria. They worked tirelessly, travelling around their colonies, making public speeches, talking and arguing and promoting the idea of federation to the general population. This, of course, was what Parkes was doing when he made his influential speech at Tenterfield—taking the argument, not to other politicians, but directly to the people of the colonies.

STEPS BACKWARDS AND FORWARDS

Far from getting excited about federation, the people of the Australian colonies, and their governments, had other things on their minds in 1891. A huge economic downturn—or depression—brought about partly by several years of bad seasons in New South Wales, a fall in the price of wool and wheat, and the failure of colonial governments and businesses to attract money from investors in Britain, hit the colonies. Many banks closed down and people lost their savings. Thousands of people lost their jobs as shops, offices and factories, unable to find the money to keep operating, closed down. Many families were forced to beg or to accept food, clothing and shelter from churches and charity groups. The discovery of gold at Coolgardie and Kalgoorlie in Western Australia in the early 1890s sent thousands of men across the Nullarbor to seek their fortunes, and saved Western Australia from the worst effects of the depression.

On top of his other problems, the political fortunes of Sir Henry Parkes went into a sudden decline. In October 1891 his government was defeated in parliament. Parkes resigned and George Dibbs, who was against federation, became premier of New South Wales. Dibbs and Parkes belonged to two opposing political groups, or parties. Dibbs was a 'protectionist', which meant he supported the use of tariffs on goods coming into New South Wales to protect the interests of farms and businesses in that colony. Parkes was a 'free-trader'. He and his supporters believed that there should be no tariffs on goods that were traded between the colonies. To make matters worse, the man who took over from Parkes as leader of the free trade group was George Reid, a man that Parkes detested, and whom he had once ridiculed as a 'barren-minded provincialist'. Parkes had his reasons to believe that Reid, like Dibbs, had little interest in federation.

Parkes stood for parliament at the elections of 1894, but failed to get elected. He died of a heart attack on 27 April 1896.

A new political party

It was not just the depression that delayed any further progress towards federation after the 1891 convention. When the draft constitution was introduced into the colonial parliaments, people began to find fault with it. In general,

People queue for food during the depression of the early 1890s.

politicians in parliament did not react with the same enthusiasm as the delegates to the convention. In New South Wales, the largest colony, the premier, George Dibbs, was opposed to any kind of federation, and the leader of the opposition, George Reid, thought that some parts of it were 'not democratic enough'. To make things more difficult, a new political party, formed in 1890, had been very successful in elections in 1891—more than a quarter of the members elected to the New South Wales Legislative Assembly in that year were members of this party. This was the Labour Electoral League, which later became the Australian Labor Party. Its members were concerned mainly about improving the conditions for workers and protecting their rights. Especially at a time when workers everywhere were losing their jobs, arguments about federation seemed not very important to the Labour League.

For the next couple of years, then, federation seemed to fade into the background as more urgent matters took centre stage.

Barton

When Parkes resigned as premier in 1891, he asked Edmund Barton to take over as leader of the federation movement in New South Wales. Barton readily accepted. Barton turned 42 in 1891. He was born and educated in Sydney and had a background as a successful lawyer. He was first elected to the New South Wales Legislative Assembly in 1879 at the age of 30, and he had been prominent at the 1891 convention in Sydney. No-one could doubt Barton's great enthusiasm for federation. However, quite a few people had doubts about his ability to promote the cause of federation effectively.

'Toby' Barton, as he was affectionately known, was a popular figure, but he had a

Barton and Deakin.

reputation for being a bit lazy. He was a scholarly man who had a great interest in ancient Greek literature, but he did not seem to hold strong political views—except about federation. He was known to have a liking for alcohol—as he put it, for 'spirits and soda'—and this earned him the nickname 'toss-pot Toby'.

Toss-pot Toby, however, surprised everyone with the vigour and energy with which he threw himself into the cause for federation, both inside and outside of parliament. In 1892, he managed to persuade the New South Wales Legislative Assembly to approve, in principle, the resolutions of the 1891 convention. Largely due to Barton's efforts, a series of organisations called 'federation leagues' sprang up around New South Wales. These were organisations which, like the Australian Natives Association, supported and publicised federation. What Barton was determined to do was to make federation a 'citizens' movement'.

In December 1892, Barton went to the Riverina, an agricultural area near the New South Wales–Victoria border, and addressed a series of meetings. As a result, no fewer than 15 federation leagues were formed in the region in early 1893. The federation league movement was firmly established in July 1893, when Barton addressed a large meeting at the Sydney Town Hall and formed the Australasian Federation League with himself as its leader.

Between 1893 and the end of the century, Barton made as many as 1000 speeches at meetings in support of federation. Even though he lost his seat in parliament in 1894, he continued his tireless public campaign.

Alfred Deakin

Nobody could have accused Alfred Deakin of being lazy or of being a drinker. This intense, deeply religious man applied himself rigorously to whatever he did—to his studies at Melbourne Grammar School and then at Melbourne University, to his early career, first as a schoolmaster, then as a lawyer, and then as a writer of newspaper articles for the Melbourne *Age*. In 1879, at the age of 23, he was elected to the

Alfred Deakin, as depicted by a cartoonist in 1908.

Victorian Legislative Assembly and remained a member right until federation. During the 1880s, he was largely responsible for introducing irrigation to the Mildura region along the Murray River and for improving the conditions of factory workers in Victoria.

During the 1890s, federation became Deakin's passion. At the age of 35, he was the youngest delegate to the federation convention of 1891. Despite the differences in their personalities and tastes, he and Barton formed a close friendship. Like Barton, he crisscrossed his colony, and indeed the whole continent, using his great gifts as a public speaker to push the cause of federation. He was a leading member of the Australian Natives Association, which was the strongest organisation supporting federation in Victoria, and was vice-president of the Australasian Federation League of Victoria when it was formed in July 1894.

After federation, he was attorney-general (the chief law officer) in Barton's first Australian government, and in 1903, when Barton retired, he became the second prime minister.

PEOPLE'S CONVENTIONS

Thanks to the efforts of people like Barton and Deakin, popular support for federation was growing. Between 31 July and 3 August 1893, the Australasian Federation League organised a 'people's conference' at Corowa, a small township in southern New South Wales on the banks of the Murray River. Here 72 invited delegates, most of them from the Federation Leagues and the Australian Natives Association, met to talk about federation. For a while, it seemed that nothing might come of this meeting except a succession of resolutions in favour of federation. As discussions went on endlessly, one delegate loudly exclaimed that all he was hearing was 'words, words, words'. 'Can't we do something?' he asked angrily.

At that, a lawyer named Robert Quick, from Bendigo in Victoria, conferred with another delegate, Robert Garran, a close associate of Edmund Barton's. They devised a motion which Quick proposed to the convention. It was to set the pattern for the future progress of the federation campaign and was to earn for the little town of Corowa the title 'birthplace of federation'. Quick's motion proposed that all the colonies should pass laws calling for a new federation convention and that all the delegates to this convention should be elected by the people. At this stage, of course, the 'people' who voted were only adult white men. The motion went further, calling for a new constitution to be written at this convention. After that, at a series of 'referendums', the people in each of the colonies would vote 'yes' or 'no' on whether they approved of this new constitution. In this way, federation, if it happened at all, would be achieved by democratic means, and not merely as a result of what members of parliaments wanted.

As we shall see, this is exactly how federation was finally agreed upon, but it still needed the cooperation of politicians to make it happen.

Bathurst

Between 16 and 21 November 1896, over 200 delegates attended a people's convention at Bathurst in western New South Wales. It was organised by the Bathurst branch of the Australasian Federation League, but included members of many different organisations. As John Quick, who was at this conference, later wrote: 'An effort was made to secure the representation of every interest, every class, and every body recognised as the mouth-piece of organised opinion.'

One of the important matters debated at Bathurst was the question of whether members of the Senate, the upper house of the Australian parliament, should be elected by the people or appointed by members of the House of Representatives. The people's convention voted strongly in favour of the people's vote. Once again, when the final version of the Australian constitution was written, the Senate was to be elected directly by the people.

George Reid

George Reid took over from Henry Parkes in 1891 as leader of the free trade group in the New South Wales parliament, and became premier in 1894. He remained premier until 1899. There is no doubt that, as premier of the colony with the largest population, he played a vital role in the achievement of federation. But, even today, there is argument about whether Reid really believed in federation. A famous Australian historian, Manning Clark, believed that everything Reid did to promote federation was motivated by the desire to become the first prime minister of the new nation. In other words, he did whatever he thought would be most popular. In March 1898, in Sydney, Reid made an amazing speech which angered federationists. He claimed to be personally in favour of it, but also pointed out that there were some good arguments against it. It was this speech that earned him the nickname 'Yes-No Reid', a name that stuck with him for the rest of his life.

Whatever the truth about Reid, ardent federationists such as Barton and Deakin did not trust him. And, as we saw earlier, Parkes detested him. As early as 1887, Reid had refused to work in a government with Parkes, because he was opposed to Parkes' ideas about federation.

George Reid was a huge man with a bushy moustache who often wore a monocle. He was known to be a great teller of jokes and funny stories. He was a gift to cartoonists, who often made fun of him in the newspapers. He could be made to look a fool, but he was no fool. Even his enemies admitted that he was shrewd and cunning. In November 1897, he was described in one newspaper as 'that astute stout gentleman with the glazed eye'. Furthermore, he was a powerful public speaker. He used his jovial manner to win over his audiences and often used rough humour to ridicule his opponents.

Decisive action

To be fair to Reid, he was in a difficult position as far as federation was concerned . There were many influential people in New South Wales, and throughout the other colonies, who bitterly opposed federation, at least in the form that it had been proposed at the 1891 convention. In 1897 in Melbourne, an anti-federation weekly newspaper, *Tocsin*, began circulating. Writers in this paper claimed that federation would take away the freedoms of individual colonies. They were also strongly opposed to the idea that the Senate should have an equal number of members from each colony, regardless of size. This, they argued—and many people agreed with them—made nonsense of the idea of 'one man, one vote'.

Late in 1894, soon after he became premier of New South Wales, Reid telegraphed all the other Australian premiers, suggesting that they meet in Hobart, mainly to discuss federation. He had been urged to do this by members of the Australasian Federation League. It was a decisive act by a man who many people criticised for being indecisive. This meeting revived the push to federation among the colonies' political leaders. It gave rise to a series of meetings, conventions and, eventually, referendums that ended with Australia becoming a sovereign nation in January 1901.

Banquet menu for the 1897 federal convention.

THE FINAL STAGES

Between March 1887 and March 1888, another federal convention was held to discuss federation . Ten delegates from each of the colonies, except Queensland, attended. As the Corowa people's convention had suggested, all the delegates, except those from Western Australia, were elected by the people of the individual colonies. The government of Western Australia insisted on appointing its delegates. In the elections for these delegates, women were able to vote for the first time, but only the women of one colony— South Australia. Thanks to the efforts of women campaigners for equal rights, South Australian women were given the right to vote in 1894. One South Australian woman, Catherine Helen Spence, even tried to get elected as a delegate to the convention, but she did not get sufficient votes.

Queensland refused to take part in this convention, partly because it feared that in a federated Australia it would be prevented from using cheap Kanaka labour on its sugar plantations, and partly because there was a strong movement in that colony for two new colonies—one in central Queensland and one in north Queensland—to be formed. If that happened, there would be no chance of bringing all three 'Queensland' colonies into a federation. New Zealand, which was no longer interested in joining with Australia, did not attend either.

Forging an agreement

The 1887–88 convention was held in three sessions and in three cities. The first session,

Catherine Helen Spence.

in Adelaide, lasted for just a month. The South Australian premier, Charles Kingston, who was strongly in favour of federation, was elected president. Edmund Barton led the New South Wales delegates, even though Reid was also there. This session ended so early because the colonial premiers were due to go to London to take part in celebrations to mark the 50th anniversary of Queen Victoria's reign. While they were there they also had discussions with Joseph Chamberlain who, as secretary of state for the colonies, had a particular interest in Australia's federation movement. Chamberlain had ideas about what should be written into the new constitution, and some of these were adopted in the final version.

A second session of the convention took place in Sydney for about three weeks in September 1897, immediately after the premiers had got back from London. The third and final session took place between January and March 1898 in Melbourne, where the weather was swelteringly hot, and where smoke from bushfires in the nearby hills made conditions extremely uncomfortable.

Throughout the whole convention, Barton impressed everyone by his energy and hard work. Any reputation for laziness was now long gone. Often he would stay up right through the night, working on a final version for the new constitution. Always, in the morning, he would be ready for the meetings, arguing eloquently and trying hard to win over delegates who disagreed with him.

Delegates to the second session of the Federal Convention.

'tyranny of distance' still applied there. The only way one could reach South Australia, the nearest colony, was by taking a long boat trip across the rough waters of the Great Australian Bight.

As a result only four colonies—New South Wales, Victoria, South Australia and Tasmania—took part in referendums that were held on 3 and 4 June 1898. In each of the four colonies, more people voted in favour of the consti-tution than against it. The total vote in favour was more than two to one. In Victoria it was almost five to one. But in New South Wales the 'yes' vote, which totalled 71 595, was just over 5000 more than the vote for 'no'. Before the referendum, the New South Wales govern-ment had ruled that the referendum would not be considered 'carried' unless at least 80 000 people in that colony voted in favour. Many people blamed Reid's 'yes-no' speech of a couple of months before, which you read about on page 57, for the loss in New South Wales. Progress towards federation had struck a barrier.

And many arguments there were. Often they were about the Senate—about what powers it would have and about the numbers of members from the different colonies it would contain. Some Victorian and New South Wales delegates were concerned that the smaller states would be able to combine in the Senate to defeat laws that favoured the two largest states.

Eventually, however, agreement was reached and a constitution was written and approved by the convention. The next step was to hold referendums in each of the colonies to see if the people, too, approved of this constitution.

Referendums

When the premier of Western Australia, the former explorer Sir John Forrest, returned from the convention, he found that his government was not prepared to agree to a referendum about federation. Many people there believed that Western Australia's population was still too small for it to compete with other states in a federation. Many Western Australians, too, felt isolated from the rest of the continent. The

More referendums

The premiers met again in Melbourne in Jan-uary 1899. This time, the premier of Queensland, J.R. Dickson, was present. The premiers argued about making changes to the constitution. One of the changes New South Wales wanted was that the capital of the country be situated there. The Victorians, in particular, were not happy about that. However, an agreement was reached that the capital would be in New South Wales, but would be situated at least 100 miles

(160 km) from Sydney. Until the new site was agreed upon and a city built, the parliament of Australia would be based in Melbourne. Some of the demands made by Queensland were also agreed to. By this time, Queenslanders in the central and northern parts began to fear that if they did not become part of the new federation, the whole colony would be dominated by Brisbane, in the south, where most of the population lived. Only Western Australia went away unsatisfied. It had demanded, among other things, that it be allowed to continue charging tariffs on goods coming in from other states, and also that the new Australian government agree to build a railway across the desert from the gold town of Kalgoorlie to Port Augusta in South Australia. The premiers would not agree to this.

New referendums now had to be held in all the colonies, except Western Australia. This time, with both Reid and Barton campaigning for a 'yes' vote, more than 107 000 people in New South Wales voted in favour of, and almost 84 000 voted against, the revised constitution. Victoria, Tasmania and South Australia once again were strongly in favour. In Queensland the majority in favour was much narrower. Now, however, all the Australian colonies except Western Australia were ready to federate.

Western Australia

As we noted earlier, there were important gold rushes in Western Australia in the 1890s, and these had brought many people streaming into that colony. While the Western Australian government remained opposed to holding a referendum, the diggers on the goldfields, most of them from the eastern colonies, began to campaign for a 'goldfields' state that would separate from Western Australia and federate with the rest of the nation. Finally the government gave in to the campaigners and, on 31 July 1900, a referendum was held in Western Australia. It was carried by a large majority.

Almost four weeks earlier, on 5 July 1900, the British parliament had passed a Bill agreeing to the formation of the new nation of Australia and approving its constitution. Western Australia, then, came very close to staying on as a British colony, outside the rest of Australia. If that had happened, Edmund Barton's dream of a 'continent for a nation and a nation for a continent' would not have been fulfilled, at least not for some time to come.

Voting in the first New South Wales referendum.

A Century Later

A hundred years after federation, the Australian system of government remains basically the same as it was in 1901. There are still six states, and each of them has an elected government that controls matters like school education, hospitals and roads and public transport. The trains or buses you use to get to school or work are the responsibility of your state government. The Australian government, which, since 1927, has been based in Canberra in the Australian Capital Territory, controls those matters that concern the whole of the Australian nation. These include the defence of the country, relations with other countries, rules that control trade between Australia and other countries, taxes and the overall control of the country's economy. The Australian government also has authority over the two parts of the country that remain 'territories'—the Australian Capital Territory, which is the area around Canberra, the national capital—and the Northern Territory. However both these territories now have their own governments which control a lot of the activities that occur within them.

Two houses of parliament

There are still two 'houses' of parliament that make up the Australian government—the House of Representatives and the Senate. The House of Representatives is often called the 'people's house', because its members are elected by the voters all over Australia. As set out in the Constitution, the Senate is officially a states' house and the people in each state elect the members of the Senate that are supposed to represent the interests of that state. The people in the Northern Territory and the Australian Capital Territory also elect some members to the Senate. As you read on page 53, only the House of Representatives has the right to introduce new laws. However, the Senate is able to suggest changes to laws that have been passed in the House of Representatives or even to refuse to approve them at all. If a majority of

New Parliament House.

members of the Senate vote against a law, then that law is not passed.

But the Senate does not really work in the way the people who drew up the Constitution intended. They saw it as a way of protecting the states against laws that might not be in their interest. However, particularly since the Liberal Party was founded in opposition to the Labor Party, party politics have dominated both houses of the Australian parliament. This means that members of the Senate, known as senators, tend to act and vote according to which political party they belong to, rather than which state they come from.

Monarchy or republic?

At the beginning of the 21st century, one of the major issues in Australia is whether the nation should become a republic. As you read earlier, the Australian Constitution states that Australia's official head of state is the queen or king of England, who is represented in Australia by the governor-general. Australia is, then, a constitutional monarchy. Many Australians now feel that the time has come to change that. They claim that Australia should have a 'president' as its official head of state, and that that president should be an Australian citizen. That means that Australia, like most other countries, including the United States, would become a republic.

The movement towards a republic gained strength in Australia through the 1980s and 1990s. The Labor prime minister, Paul Keating, strongly promoted this movement. When Labor was defeated in elections in 1996, the Liberal leader John Howard, who opposed a republic, became prime minister. He campaigned against it, even though it seemed that most Australians now wanted their own head of state. In 1999, a referendum was held to determine whether Australia would enter the 21st century as a republic with an Australian as head of state. Although the result was close, most people voted 'no', and Australia remains a monarchy.

However, this does not simply mean that the majority of Australians wanted Australia to

Members of the Republican Movement converge at the Sydney Opera House steps in 1999.

remain a monarchy. There is no doubt that many people who were strongly in favour of a republic voted 'no' in this referendum. They were not voting 'no' to a republic, they were voting 'no' to a president chosen by the combined members of the House of Representatives and the Senate, which was the model being voted on in the referendum. These people, called 'direct electionists', wanted a president elected directly by the people of Australia, and not by members of parliament.

It is likely that Australians will again vote on becoming a republic. As many members of all political parties, and most Labor members, are in favour of it, it is possible that before very much longer, Australia will have a prime minister and a leader of the opposition who will both favour a republic. When that happens, the move towards a republic will no doubt gain new strength.

INDEX